WINE
UNCORKED

WINE
UNCORKED

FIONA BECKETT

WILLOW CREEK PRESS

Wine Uncorked

By Fiona Beckett

Published in the USA by Willow Creek Press, Inc.
P. O. Box 147, Minocqua, WI 54548
For information on other Willow Creek titles,
call 1-800-850-9453

First published in Great Britain in 1999 by Mitchell
Beazley, an imprint of Octopus Publishing
Group Ltd., Michelin House, 81 Fulham Road,
London SW3 6RB.

Senior Editor: Lucy Bridgers
Special photography: James Johnson, Ray Moller
Picture Research: Claire Gouldstone
Production: Paul Hammond, Karen Farquhar
Index: Anne Barrett

ISBN 1 57223 201 3

Printed in China

Contents

Introduction

The wine world has changed out of all recognition in the last few years. The range of bottles is wider than ever before. New countries such as Argentina and Chile have arrived on the scene, while traditional winegrowing regions such as the Languedoc have reinvented themselves. The choice is sometimes overwhelming.

Although specialist wine shops and restaurants are much friendlier and more welcoming than they used to be, dealing with a subject about which you feel you know very little can still be intimidating. The worry about mispronouncing names and choosing a wine that disappoints your guests can set a meal off to an edgy start. But it doesn't have to be this way.

People for whom wine-drinking is a way of life aren't beset by these anxieties. Go to a restaurant in France or Italy and they often plunk a carafe of wine down on the table. No one would dream of drinking a wine that came from another region let alone another country. Drinking wine is as natural as drinking water.

In our anxiety about labels and vintages we sometimes lose sight of the fact that wine is supposed to be enjoyable. That's why I've devoted so much space in this book to entertaining and matching wine with food. Buying wine to share with friends, choosing a bottle for a special celebration – even simply picking a wine to match your mood – this should be what winedrinking is all about.

Of course there are useful tips, too, that can help you along the way. Information about how long you can store wine for, at what temperature to serve it, and how you can tell if something's wrong with it. What kind of glasses to use, what corkscrew to choose and how to open a Champagne bottle without damaging the paintwork. If I've assumed you know less than you do I apologize. All I can say is it took me ages to learn this kind of stuff.

As you begin to discover the wine world there's plenty more to satisfy your curiosity. If you've developed a taste for barrel-fermented Chardonnay, for instance, you can find out in the Wine Styles section what other wines are made in a similar style, and in the Grapes section which countries are best at producing it. If you find you're constantly drawn to the wines of a country such as Australia or California you can check in the regional guide what else that country has to offer. You can even find out why that Chardonnay tastes the way it does by reading the sections on what goes on in the vineyard and in the winery, and about the effects of different oak treatments. In short, feel free to dip in. Read as much or as little as you like.

But if there's one part of the book I believe is more important than any other it's the practical tastings. Truly there's no better or more enjoyable way to get to know wine. So often our attitude toward wine is based on prejudice and ignorance. You only have to think about how poor an image a grape such as Riesling has, yet when people who haven't drunk it before actually try it they usually love it. Never pass up an opportunity to try something you haven't tasted before.

So *Wine Uncorked* isn't just about explaining the mysteries of wine, though I hope it does and that you find it helpful. It's fundamentally an invitation to get out that corkscrew, open a bottle and participate in one of the great pleasures the world has to offer. And you don't have to be a millionaire to do it with style.

The flavor wheel

When you first start tasting wine you may find its complex flavors difficult to describe. Indeed the terms wine writers use – such as buttery or toasty – may make little sense. To help you recognize the wines you like I have included a flavor wheel* throughout this book, which pinpoints some of the more common flavors you might find.

At the heart of the wheel are general descriptions you may already be familiar with, such as "fruity." But being able to identify what kind of fruit a wine tastes of will help you relate it to other wines you've tried. Around the outside of the wheel you'll find the full spectrum of flavors. They're arranged in order of intensity – the citrus and tropical flavors being more typical of white wines, the richer red-berry and dried-fruit flavors more common to reds.

This approach will help you identify the flavors that make up even the most complex wines. Wines that are savory, for instance, have a lot more going on in them than simple fruit flavors, even though you might find it hard to pin down what that is. But keep swirling the wine around and you may find it smells and tastes like one of the more specific flavors I've picked out, such as truffles.

The wheel is particularly useful in highlighting the differences in wines made from the same grape variety. In the grape tasting sections you'll see that all the wines have their own wheel, revealing their similarities but also their differences. For instance, most Cabernets taste of blackcurrant, but not all taste of cedar or tobacco (*see* pages 70–1).

The wheels can also help you focus on the subtle flavors of wines. If you've never tasted a wine such as Chablis before, you might be hard pressed to get beyond the fact that it's dry. But if I suggest that it's almost mineral in flavor and that the fruit is more crisp apple and lemon than the ripe peach flavor of other Chardonnays, it helps to fix it in your mind.

* The idea of a flavor wheel was first developed by staff at the Department of Viticulture and Enology at the University of California at Davis (see page 144).

Examples of how the flavor wheel works

Australian Cabernet Sauvignon

Here there are only a few flavors, but that doesn't mean the wine is uninteresting. Australian Cabernets, particularly those from the Coonawarra region, have a very intense character dominated by sweet blackcurrant fruit and minty eucalyptus, picked up from the eucalyptus trees surrounding the vineyards. The oak is simply there as a support to make sure the wine has the potential for ageing (*see* also pages 70–1).

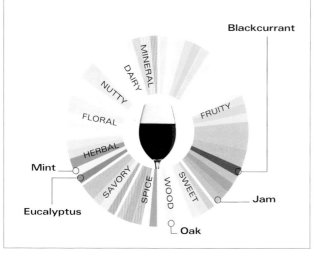

Chablis

Chablis might appear to be a very straightforward style of wine, but its apparently neutral flavors disguise a great deal of complexity. Young Chablis may remind you of flint, stones and tart green apples, but keep it for six months or longer and you will start to pick up other flavors such as lemon and cream. More expensive, oaked Premier Cru Chablis will be even richer.

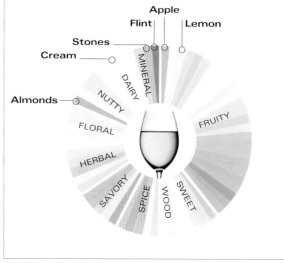

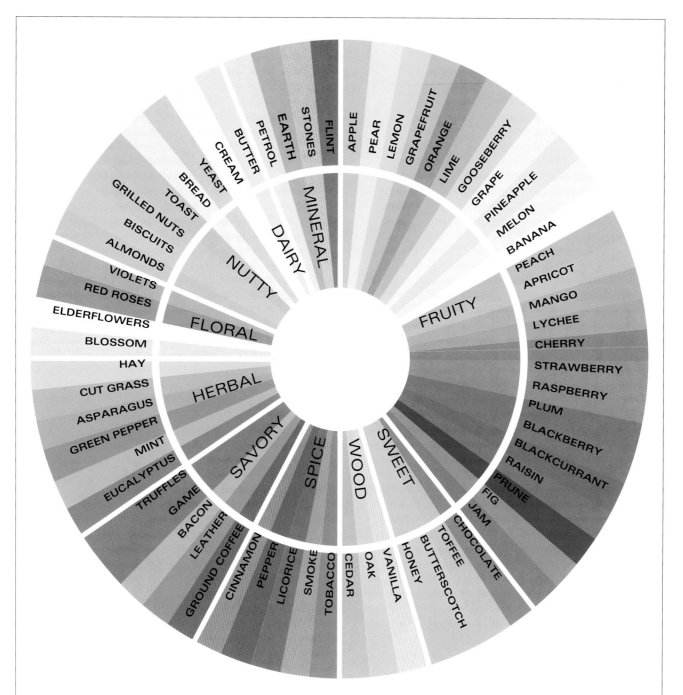

How to use the flavor wheel

Decorative though it is, the wheel is more than a glorious kaleidoscope of color. The flavors have been arranged carefully starting with the most neutral, such as flint and stones, at the top of the wheel, working around to the most intense, such as pepper and licorice. Inside the wheel you'll find the main flavor groups, such as fruity and floral – descriptions of wine that you may find used in their own right. But if you want to know what specific type of fruit or flower a wine tastes of you can find it on the outer ring. The wheel is used throughout the book with the key flavors highlighted so they're easy to recognize. If you're attracted to certain flavors such as citrus, or are less keen on others such as oak, look for them on the wheels. You can also find a key to the flavors on the wheel on pages 136–7.

Finding the wines you like

When you think how different our tastes are in food, it's hardly surprising that we like different wines. Yet because most of us understand less about wine than food, we are far more likely to allow ourselves to be browbeaten into drinking a wine we don't really enjoy.

What determines the wines we like is partly our physical makeup and partly a question of what kind of taste experiences we've been exposed to. Some people have much more sensitive palates than others and can pick up flavors that other people wouldn't even notice.

If you've been drinking wine for a number of years, you're likely to be more tolerant of a wide variety of different wines than if you've only ever tasted one or two. Offbeat flavors can seem intriguing and complex; other people might think these wines are faulty. You might find it difficult to articulate what it is that you like about the wines you enjoy. It may be easier to describe what you dislike about the wines that don't appeal to you. Here are some characteristics that are likely to attract you or put you off certain wine styles.

Sharpness

Do you like the sensation you get when you bite into a crisp green apple? How do you react to unsweetened lemon juice? These sharp (some would say sour) flavors are more common in whites than reds – particularly those from cooler, more northerly parts of France and Italy. If you like these flavors go for crisp, dry whites and lighter unoaked reds.

Smoothness/softness

This is one of the most highly prized qualities in wine, which accounts for the enormous popularity of Chardonnay and soft, medium-bodied reds such as Merlot. Most winemakers these days strive to make their wines smooth and easy to drink. Winemakers from warmer winegrowing countries and regions such as Australia or the south of France, find it easiest to do so. If you like smooth wines you're most likely to find them among medium-bodied styles.

Oakiness

A wine can be oaked without you being able to detect it (particularly if it is an older wine), but when you smell vanilla, grilled nuts or toast in a wine, rather than simple fruit aromas, then the oak becomes obvious. Often this is combined with quite high levels of alcohol, so you get a spicy aftertaste when you swallow. If you like this kind of wine look for full-bodied whites and reds. If you prefer this less, remember that getting rid of overly oaky flavors can simply be a question of keeping the wine long enough for them to integrate.

Fruitiness

Your attitude to fruitiness in wine often depends on the type of wine to which you were first introduced. If you started with New-World wines, you'll probably like wines that have a lot of fruit flavor and find more traditional wines a bit thin. If you were brought up on French wine, you may well find Australian or Californian wines too jammy. But it's not a pure European versus New World divide. Even in France winemakers now make their wines in a far more fruity style.

Sweetness

We all recognize a sweet wine when we come across one but how dry is dry? Technically, dry whites range from Muscadet, which is very dry and minerally, to an Australian Chardonnay or Colombard, which can taste quite sweet. If you like the former go for a crisp, dry white. If you prefer the latter, try a medium- or full-bodied one. And if you'd rather drink a wine that's got some obvious sweetness, go for one that is medium-dry or *demi-sec*.

Floweriness/spiciness

This is a quality that's more common in whites. Certain grape varieties – such as Riesling or Torrontes – have a pronounced aromatic character that tends to strongly polarize wine drinkers for and against them. They mainly appeal to people who have more winedrinking experience. (*See* pages 14–5.)

Maturity

With time the simple fruit or fruit-and-oak flavors you get in young wines disappear and more complex flavors develop. If these appeal to you read the section on ageing and vintages (pages 86–8).

Over the next few pages you'll be able to discover what the most common wines are in each style.

White wine styles

Above: Crisp, zesty Sauvignon Blanc.

Crisp, fresh dry whites

Crisp, fresh, clean and citrussy: there are times when you want a glass of cold white wine and nothing else will do. Most inexpensive whites come into this category – especially those from cooler parts of France, Spain and Italy. Look to these wines for your everyday drinking.

Sauvignon Blanc

Wines made from the Sauvignon grape are the zingiest, zestiest, most citrussy of all. The most intense flavors come from the New World – particularly the Marlborough region of New Zealand; the finest, most delicate minerally flavors are found in classic Loire Sauvignons such as Sancerre and Pouilly-Fumé. Other Sauvignon hotspots are South Africa, Hungary, parts of Spain and Italy and Bordeaux, often labeled simply as Bordeaux Blanc (*see also* pages 63, 93). And many other inexpensive whites such as Vin de Pays des Côtes de Gascogne are made in a similarly crisp, lemony style.

Italian whites

It's easy to overlook Italian whites. They're not made from well-known grapes. They can be neutral to the point of blandness. But they're some of the most versatile, easy-drinking and (fashionable wines like Gavi apart) inexpensive dry whites around. The best-known are Pinot Grigio (the name of both the wine and the grape), Soave (slightly fuller and nuttier) and Frascati (often fruitier). Others to look for are Bianco di Custoza, which is quite similar to Soave (and from the same region, the Veneto) and Umbria's classic Orvieto. Also try some of the new-wave whites from southern Italy and Sicily.

Muscadet and other French dry whites

Muscadet is still one of the driest of dry whites, even though it is less sharply acidic than it once was. Look for the words *sur lie* on the label, indicating that the wine has been kept on its flavorsome lees (*see* page 81). In most other regions of France dry white wines tend to be just that, except in the Languedoc, where many *vins de pays* are made in a fruitier New World style. Most inexpensive white burgundies, such as Mâcon Blanc and Petit Chablis, are also steelier and less creamy than their pricier counterparts.

Where else to look
With super-efficient modern technology, countries that were never noted for their white wines are suddenly producing some crisp, fresh, quaffable examples. Spain is one (especially the zesty whites of Rueda), Portugal another. Other countries such as England and Germany, more noted for their inexpensive, medium-dry whites, have switched to a drier style.

Smooth dry whites

The most popular style of white wine by far, this smooth, creamy style of white has no rasping acidity or overtly oaky character to surprise the unwary drinker. Smooth and mellow, they slip down as easily on their own as they do with food. Most of the big-selling branded wines are made in this style – basically a wine with which it's hard to go wrong.

Chablis

This is probably the dry white wine most people could name, though they don't always realize it comes from Burgundy or even that it's made from Chardonnay. In fact, Chablis ranges hugely in style from very sharp, crisp, lean young wines to the much richer, more honeyed style of a Premier or

Tasting wheel

Wine: Soave
Style: crisp, fresh, dry whites
Dominant flavors:
stones
cream
almonds
lemon

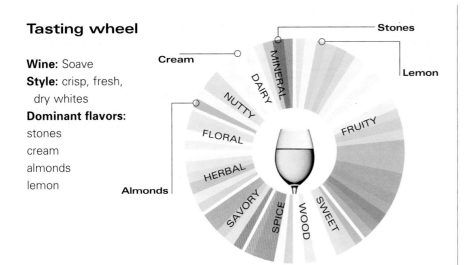

Grand Cru. Most bottles will be very dry by the standard of most white wines today: not overly fruity but with more of an elegant, steely, flinty character (*see* page 61). Other basic to medium-priced white burgundies such as Bourgogne Blanc, Mâcon-Villages and St-Véran are made in a similar style.

Chardonnay

If you like this style of wine you're bound to end up drinking Chardonnay. It's made by virtually every wine-producing country at every kind of price. So how do you tell whether it's a smooth, creamy type of Chardonnay or a big full-bodied oaky one? Well price is a guide (the cheaper it is the less likely it is to be full-bodied), but the key is whether or not it is aged in oak barrels. If the label says "Unoaked" or "Unwooded" then it will be made in a lighter, fruitier style. If it says "Barrel Matured", "Barrel Fermented" or "Reserve" then it will taste toastier and oakier (*see* pages 82–4).

Alternatives to Chardonnay

As an alternative to Chardonnay, you may prefer slightly drier whites or ones that have more obviously fruity flavors.

If you like drier whites, try traditional southern French whites such as Côtes du Rhône, better-quality Italian whites such as Lugana and Soave Classico, Pinot Blanc (also known as Pinot Bianco), California Fumé Blanc, White Bordeaux and other oaked Sauvignon and Sémillon and South African Chenin Blanc.

Lovers of fruitier whites should try exuberant, flavorsome Australian whites such as Semillon-Chardonnay and Colombard. Interesting wines are also being made (mainly in Australia at present) with the luscious, lime-flavored grape Verdelho, and, in New Zealand and on the West Coast of the US, with Pinot Gris, which produces delicate, slightly peachy wines.

Rich, full-bodied whites

Can a white wine be full-bodied? Yes it can – though obviously not in the big, beefy style of a full-bodied red. Full-bodied whites are not so much refreshing as intense and richly satisfying, best for drinking with food rather than on their own. Usually (though not always) that richness is due to oak-ageing. And almost invariably it involves the Chardonnay grape.

Tasting wheel

Wine: Unoaked Chardonnay
Style: smooth, dry whites
Dominant flavors:
apple
melon
lemon
peach
mango

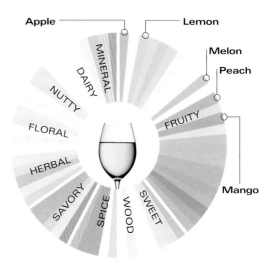

Tasting wheel

Wine: Californian
  barrel-fermented
  Chardonnay
Style: rich,
full-bodied whites
Dominant flavors:
lemon
melon
peach
mango
butterscotch
oak
toast

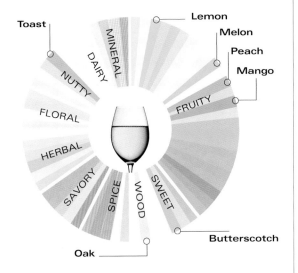

Chardonnay

Apologies to those who feel they've
had enough of Chardonnay, but there's
no getting away from it: this is the
world's most important white grape
and a large proportion of the best white
wines are made from it. The more
affordable wines (from Eastern Europe,
South Africa, Australia and increasingly
Argentina) owe almost all their
character to being matured in toasty oak
barrels. They are not subtle but they're
packed with flavor. More expensive
wines – fine white burgundies such as
Premier Cru Chablis and Puligny-
Montrachet and top Chardonnays from
Australia, California and New Zealand –
are more refined. They may be kept in
oak for longer but the oak flavor is more
integrated; the effect is a wonder-fully
rich, creamy texture and a long,
lingering aftertaste (*see also* pages 82–4).

Australian Semillon

Australian Semillon can be
surprisingly low in alcohol for a
full-bodied wine, and, drunk within
the first year or two, it simply tastes
fresh, crisp and fruity. But, despite the
fact that many Semillons are unoaked,
they develop over time an
extraordinarily intense, luscious
roast pineapple flavor that brings
them firmly into the full-bodied camp.
(Sometimes producers will get this
effect more quickly by maturing
the wine in oak barrels.) A similar
wine is Marsanne, a white-wine
grape originally from the Rhône
that has found a natural home in
the state of Victoria.

Hermitage and other traditional Rhône whites

The Rhône produces impressively
full-bodied whites from local grapes,
such as Marsanne and Roussanne,
to match the region's powerful reds.
These aren't always the easiest
wines to develop a taste for. When
they're young they can be quite
austere and lacking in fruit, but
after several years' ageing they
become quite magnificent.

Where else to look

Other curiosities in this style are
Jurancon Sec and Pacherenc du Vic-
Bilh, two spicy, full-bodied wines
from the southwest of France that
are usually a good buy if you find
them on a restaurant wine list. You
could also try a traditional white
Rioja which has received extended
oak ageing.

Fragrant aromatic whites

If you're looking for something
different, this is where to find it.
They might not be the kind of
wines you'd want to drink every
day, or the easiest wines to match
with food, but as an aperitif they're
hard to beat.

Riesling

Although Riesling is one of the
world's great grapes, it's suffered from
being associated with the poor quality
of many cheap, medium-dry German
whites. Ironically though, it is still
Germany that makes some of the best,
most thrillingly racy examples (*see*
pages 57–8 and 64–5). A good starting
point are those from Australia (rich
and limey) and New Zealand (slightly
fruitier and more floral).

Gewürztraminer and other spicy whites

It smells of old fashioned red roses.
It tastes of lychees and Turkish delight.
I can't guarantee you'll take to it, but
Gewürztraminer is the most exotic
wine-drinking experience you'll ever
have. Some good examples come from
New Zealand, South Africa and Chile,
but without doubt the best come from
Alsace where the umlaut (ü) is not

used (*see* page 101). Cheaper whites in this style come from countries such as Hungary, Bulgaria, Slovenia and the Czech Republic, which have a number of indigenous grape varieties with a floral, spicy character. These include Furmint, Hárslevelü, Irsai Oliver and Muscat (which is also found in the south of France).

Viognier

Viognier has become a bit of a cult grape, though few winemakers manage to produce the extraordinarily lush apricot-scented wines that emerge from its expensive northern Rhône heartland, Condrieu. But you can find some delicately scented examples from the Languedoc and some very intense ones in California, where they sometimes reach over 14 percent alcohol. A good alternative is Albariño from the Rías Baixas region of northern Spain, which has a similar peachy aroma.

Dry or medium-dry?

You might think if a bottle said "Dry white" the wine inside it would be dry. Well, not always. Cheaper white wines from countries such as Australia, New Zealand and Argentina are often given a bit of a lift by the addition of an aromatic grape variety such as Muscat, Müller-Thurgau or Torrontes, which make them taste quite flowery. Words to look for on the back label are "fragrant" and "aromatic". If you find they're not quite sweet enough for your taste look for wines labeled medium-dry, *demi-sec*, or *halbtrocken*. These include most inexpensive German wines, such as Liebfraumilch and Hock, *demi-sec* Vouvray and English medium-dry whites.

Tasting wheel

Wine:
Gerwürztraminer
Style: fragrant, aromatic whites
Dominant flavors:
lychee
pear
red roses

Above: German Riesling Kabinett and Alsace Gewurztraminer in distinctive flute bottles.

Red wine styles

Light, fruity reds

There are times when you just want a straightforward, uncomplicated, gluggable red. This is where to find it. Your main hunting grounds will be France and Italy, but most inexpensive, unoaked New-World reds are also made in a soft, fruity style. Look for bottles of 12 percent alcohol or less.

Beaujolais

The most famous fruity red of all, Beaujolais is renowned for its vivid, juicy red-berry fruit – though not all of it is as bright and bubblegummy as a Beaujolais Nouveau. More expensive "cru" Beaujolais such as Morgon and Moulin-à-Vent can be quite full-bodied. If you like Beaujolais look for other wines made from the Gamay grape such as Gamay de Touraine.

Pinot Noir

Even when it's quite high in alcohol fragrant, raspberry-scented Pinot Noir is a grape that still tends to taste light and fruity – particularly when it's young or when it's grown in a cooler region such as Burgundy. Wines in this style include basic Bourgogne Rouge, and cheaper Pinots from Spain, Chile and California.

Côtes du Rhône and other inexpensive southern French reds

The lightest of the reds from the Rhône, there's an appealing warm, sweet strawberry jam character to Côtes du Rhône, though it does vary quite markedly from vintage to vintage. Other inexpensive French reds such as Côtes du Roussillon, Coteaux du Tricastin, Côtes de Ventoux and cheap *vin de pays* share the same enjoyably quaffable character.

Valpolicella and other light Italian reds

The combination of vivid cherry-flavored fruit and crisp acidity that you get in Valpolicella is typical of inexpensive Italian reds (Bardolino and Montepulciano d'Abruzzo are two others). By modern (ie New World) standards they taste quite sharp but they really come into their own with Italian food.

Inexpensive New-World reds

Although most New-World reds tend to be medium- or full-bodied, the cheaper ones offer appealingly soft, fruity drinking. Look for basic Australian, Chilean or Argentinian reds or cheaper South African wines such as Cinsault.

Where else to look

As a general rule red wines from predominantly white-wine producing countries and regions fall into this category. Try reds from countries such as Austria, Hungary, Germany and Switzerland, and the stylish red wines of the Loire region of France, such as Chinon and Bourgueil.

Medium-bodied reds

Most of the world's well-known reds are made in a medium-bodied style. The choice is between more traditional wines such as claret and Chianti and

Above: Gamay – deliciously juicy and fruity.

more exuberantly fruity ones from the New World. What they share is a smooth, easy-drinking character without the marked acidity that characterizes lighter reds or the robust, oaky character you can find in more full-bodied wines.

Bordeaux

Bordeaux is such a huge region and the wine there made at such a wide range of prices that it's hard to generalize about style. But in truth, most of the wines that you and I are able to afford aren't going to be the lush, full-bodied *Crus Classés* (*see* pages 92–3). Inexpensive Bordeaux ranges from the simple and blackcurranty to the smoother, oak-aged wines that reflect the part of the region they come from (softer and fruitier from Merlot-dominated St-Emilion, leaner and more tannic from the Cabernet-dominated Médoc). A good vintage such as 1995 will also produce a more generously fruity wine than a lighter one, such as 1997. Similar wines to Bordeaux are made in surrounding areas such as Bergerac, Buzet, Côtes de Duras, Côtes du Frontonnais and Côtes du Marmandais (*see* pages 92–3).

Merlot

There's a soft voluptuous quality to Merlot, which makes it incredibly easy to drink. The mainstay of St-Emilion and Pomerol, it's also successfully grown in the Languedoc region of France, Spain, Italy, Hungary, South Africa and Chile. Only larger-than-life Californian Merlots tend to be really full-bodied.

Chianti

Chianti varies so much in quality that it's always difficult to predict quite what style of wine you're going to get. On the whole avoid cheaper wines and go for Chianti Classico or Chianti Rufina. This should guarantee a rich plummy wine (almost raisiny in older vintages), though always with the marked acidity typical of Italian wines. Other medium-bodied Italian reds are Barbera and Sangiovese, two grapes that aree also grown in Calfornia and Argentina.

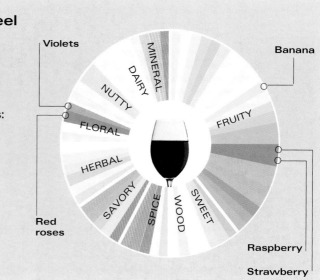

Tasting wheel

Wine: Beaujolais

Style: light, fruity reds

Dominant flavors:
strawberry
raspberry
violets
red roses
banana

Rioja

Although her reds can be quite full-bodied, Spain's best-known wine, Rioja, is soft and smooth with a sweet strawberry jam character. This partly comes from the Tempranillo grape and partly from extended barrel ageing. Younger *Joven* and *Crianza* Riojas (*see* page 112) are fruitier and more robust than their *Reserva* and *Gran Reserva* counterparts.

Crozes-Hermitage

Some of the lesser-known reds from the Rhône, such as Crozes-Hermitage, Lirac, and Vacqueyras, are smooth and fruity, but always with that slightly spicy, peppery character you get from the Syrah grape. These can be good value for the money compared with more famous wines, such as Hermitage and Châteauneuf-du-Pape.

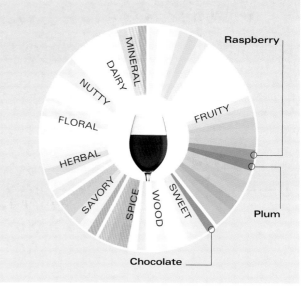

Tasting wheel

Wine: Merlot

Style: medium-bodied reds

Dominant flavors:
raspberry
plum
chocolate

Where else to look

Better quality (and inevitably more expensive) examples of lighter wines such as Valpolicella, Beaujolais, Burgundy and other New-World Pinot Noirs are generally richer and fuller than their cheaper counterparts. Most of the well-known brands of Australian wines are medium-bodied, as are the new-wave, less traditional Spanish and Portuguese reds. Try, too, the lighter Cabernet Sauvignons from South Africa, New Zealand and the Languedoc.

Full-bodied reds

Once smitten by full-bodied reds you will never look back. They are so opulent and richly flavored that they make other wines seem pale by comparison. On the whole they're the product of hotter countries and wine-growing regions such as the Rhône, Australia and California, of older vines and of extended oak ageing – which unfortunately tends to make them quite expensive.

The big red grapes

Certain grapes lend themselves to making big wines, most notably Shiraz (or Syrah), Cabernet Sauvignon and Grenache. Others, such as Californian Zinfandel and South African Pinotage, tend to be specialities of just the one country. Since these grapes are also used to make lighter styles of wine it's important to check the alcohol content on the label. Full-bodied reds tend to be 13 percent or over (14 percent plus is really powerful).

The Rhône

The Rhône is the original home of robust reds and still makes some of the

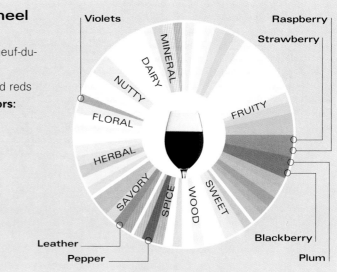

Tasting wheel

Wine: Châteauneuf-du-Pape
Style: full-bodied reds
Dominant flavors:
strawberry
raspberry
blackberry
plum
violets
pepper
leather

most dense, concentrated wines available, mainly based on the Syrah grape. Most of the bigger wines are found in the north in appellations such as Cornas, Hermitage and St-Joseph.

Wines from the southern Rhône are generally lighter in style than northern Rhône wines, with the notable exception of Châteauneuf-du-Pape. Similar styles of wines are also produced in Provence (an example is Bandol) and the Languedoc in appellations such as Fitou, St-Chinian and Pic St-Loup.

Australia

It is Australia which has wetted the world's appetite for big reds, though its wines have a sweetness and intensity of fruit that often make them seem less alcoholic than they really are. Most come from South Australia, particularly the Barossa Valley, McLaren Vale and Coonawarra (which is noted for its distinctively minty style of Cabernet Sauvignon).

Barolo, Barbaresco and other beefy Italian reds

The Italians have traditionally made some of the world's leading full-bodied reds – Barolo and Barbaresco in Piedmont, Amarone (an intense almost port-like version of Valpolicella) and the so-called super-Tuscans, Italy's equivalent to top Bordeaux. A cheaper source is southern Italy, which produces a highly individual style of raisiny red such as Aglianico del Vulture and Salice Salentino.

Where else to look

Basically, expensive reds from any country and any producer are likely to be full-bodied – what you're paying for is all that concentration and staying power. But there are cheaper alternatives if you enjoy this style of wine. They include Romanian and Moroccan reds (not subtle but satisfying), traditional Spanish and Portuguese reds from areas such as Jumilla, Ribera del Duero and the Douro, and Argentinian Malbec.

Rosé wine styles

For a long time dismissed as a totally unserious wine, rosé (which is made from red-wine grapes) is enjoying a bit of a comeback thanks largely to some particularly gutsy examples from the south of France and the New World. In fact, it makes ideal summer drinking and in many parts of Europe is drunk in preference to white wine. Two things to remember about rosé are to drink it young and to drink it cold. And the darker the color, the more powerful the wine is likely to be.

Southern France and Spain

Rosé drinking is a lifestyle in Provence, ranging from the cult Bandol, Bellet and Palette to the simple quaffing wines you find in beachside cafés. The neighboring Rhône also boasts Tavel, the only French appellation to make nothing but rosé wine. But similar robust rosés can be found more easily in the Languedoc and parts of Spain such as Navarra and Rioja (where it's called *rosado*).

Bordeaux rosé

This is a more elegant dinner party-style of rosé generally based on Merlot, which gives it a particularly soft, sweet, raspberryish character. Less common but more traditional are rosés labeled *clairet*, which are more like a light red.

Pinot Noir rosé

A speciality of the Loire (Sancerre) and of Marsannay in Burgundy, Pinot Noir has the particularly delicate, raspberry-scented fruit which you find in a cooler growing region. Expensive and elegant.

New World rosé

Rosé isn't a type of wine that's proved particularly popular in the New World but the few that are made – particularly in Australia and Argentina – have extremely lively fruit flavors. Grapes used include Grenache, Syrah and Cabernet Sauvignon, all resulting in gutsy full-flavored wines. European countries and regions that mimic the

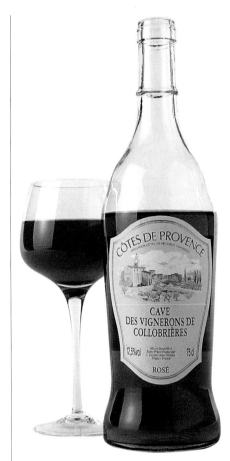

Above: Rosé – the perfect summer drink.

New World, such as Hungary and the Languedoc, also make so-called varietal wines (from a single grape variety) in a similar style.

Medium-dry rosé

The type of rosé that for a long time gave it a bad name, too many tasted like pink sugar water. But the quality of wines such as Rosé d'Anjou is slowly improving. Also immensely popular, particularly in the USA, are medium-dry "blush" wines such as white Zinfandel. And there's a growing market for sparkling off-dry rosés from Australia and from Spain.

Tasting wheel

Wine: Provençal Rosé
Style: robust rosé
Dominant flavors:
cherry
strawberry
raspberry

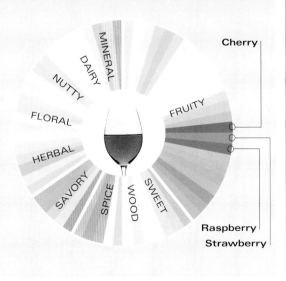

Sweet wine styles

Given that most people have a sweet tooth, it's curious how unfashionable sweet wines are. Maybe it's a legacy from the days when medium-dry and sweet wines were regarded as unsophisticated. But it means that people miss out on some of the most delicious treats the wine world has to offer.

Sweet wines are surprisingly varied in style, with flavors that range from honey and citrus to toffee and Christmas pudding. Which appeals to you depends on just how sweet-toothed you are – whether you're the kind of person who can work their way through a box of chocolates in one sitting or feels sated after one or two.

Unlike dry wines where the alcohol content is generally the most useful guide to the intensity of a wine, with sweet wines price is a better indicator. Wines that have simply been sweetened with a little grape juice (such as inexpensive German Auslese) or fortified with spirit (such as Muscat de Beaumes de Venise) are generally less sweet than wines such as Sauternes, or Trockenbeerenauslese, whose production is painstaking, expensive and time consuming.

Most of the better sweet wines are made from late-picked or late-harvested grapes that have acquired a naturally high level of sweetness. And the finest are those, like Sauternes, which are affected by a fungus called botrytis, which shrivels the grapes and concentrates the juice to a luscious intensity. These wines are often referred to as "botrytised" or as having been affected by "noble rot."

Sweet wines are generally made from white-grape varieties, principally Riesling (especially in Germany and Austria), Sémillon (Bordeaux), Chenin Blanc (the Loire) and Muscat (the world over). Most will keep – and in fact drink better – after several years.

Light and sweet

If you're trying dessert wines for the first time, the lighter styles of sweet wines are probably most likely to

Below: Lush, toffee-like liqueur Muscat.

appeal to you. These include most of the southern French Muscats such as Muscat de Beaumes-de-Venise, Spanish Moscatel de Valencia, the less expensive wines of the Loire region of France such as Coteaux du Layon and Vouvray and sweet Bordeaux (*see* opposite).

Rich and sweet

Most of the late-harvested wines from the New World tend to be quite sweet but also, as you'd expect, quite fruity too. More expensive late-harvested wines from Europe (sweet Spätlese and Auslese, *vendange tardive* wines from Alsace, and finer wines of the Loire such as Bonnezeaux and Quarts de Chaume) also come into this category, as do Italian sweet wines such as Vin Santo and Passito di Pantelleria and the great Hungarian wine Tokay (*see* page 119).

Intensely sweet

Finally there are ultra-sweet wines, hand selected from super-ripe grapes. So concentrated they're almost syrupy, they can last for decades. They include German and Austrian Beerenauslese, Trockenbeerenauslese and Eiswein or Icewine (which is made from frozen grapes and is incredibly expensive).

Red and sweet

Sweet red wines are a bit of a curiosity but make a good talking point at a dinner party. They're also one of the few wines that work well with chocolate. If you want to experiment with them a good wine to start with is Mavrodaphne of Patras, an inexpensive but delicious Greek dessert wine.

Others are Recioto della Valpolicella, South African Muscadels, the port-like Banyuls, Maury, Rasteau and Rivesaltes from southern France and of course, port itself (*see* pages 116–7).

Some contrasting examples of sweet wines to compare:
Moscatel de Valencia
Light, fragrant, grapey sometimes with a hint of orange, Moscatel de Valencia is one of the best-value dessert wines available. It should be drunk young and fresh.

Similar wines

Southern French Muscats such as Muscat de Frontignan, Muscat de Rivesaltes and Muscat de Beaumes-de-Venise.

Sauternes

The most famous sweet wine in the world. The simple citrus and honey flavors you find when the wine is young will mature into more complex nutty, dried-fruit flavors with age.

Tasting wheel

Wine: Liqueur Muscat
Dominant flavors:
toffee
butterscotch
raisin
fig

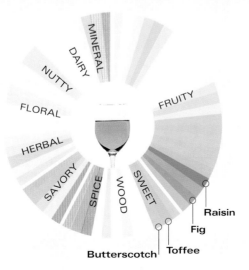

Tasting wheel

Wine: Sauternes
Dominant flavors:
lemon
honey
dried apricots
figs
hazelnuts

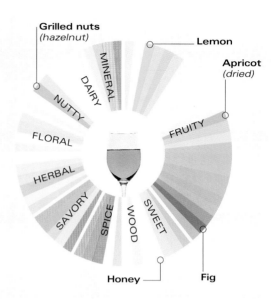

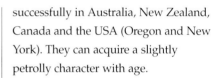

Similar wines

At a similar higher price level, Barsac. Cheaper alternatives are Premières Côtes de Bordeaux (and the individual appellations of Cadillac, Loupiac and Ste-Croix-du-Mont) and Monbazillac.

New World Late-harvest Riesling

This style of wine is widely made throughout the New World, most successfully in Australia, New Zealand, Canada and the USA (Oregon and New York). They can acquire a slightly petrolly character with age.

Similar wines

If you like this rich, lush style of sweet wine you'll probably enjoy late-harvest or botrytised Sémillons, too (some good examples come from Australia). German Spätlese Rieslings are slightly lighter and sharper; Alsace *vendange tardive* Rieslings are spicier and taste rather more exotic.

Liqueur Muscat

A speciality of the Rutherglen region in Australia – rich, lush, toffeed liqueur Muscat is almost more like a tawny port than a dessert wine.

Similar wines

Nothing quite matches liqueur Muscat for sheer fudginess, but you might well enjoy other dark Muscats such as Setúbal (Portugal); sweet oloroso sherries and Malmsey Madeira.

Sparkling wine styles

Above: The sheer elegance and style of Champagne is often hard to beat.

There was a time when virtually all sparkling wines modeled themselves on Champagne. Nowadays there's much more variety, even within the Champagne region itself, a fact that surprises many people who are under the impression that it all tastes much the same.

Unlike other wines that come from a single harvest, most Champagne is blended from wines from different years (this is what the term non-vintage means). The character of these Champagnes varies from producer to producer depending principally on which grapes are used. If Chardonnay dominates, the resulting Champagne will be lighter and more creamy (a 100-percent Chardonnay Champagne is called a *blanc de blancs*). If there is more Pinot Noir or Pinot Meunier – both dark-skinned grapes – it will be more full-bodied and toasty. Champagne made only from these grapes is called a *blanc de noirs*.

The style of non-vintage Champagne also reflects its price. An inexpensive Champagne will be quite light and even acidic. A more expensive one from a high-quality producer such as Bollinger or Roederer will be more full-bodied.

Vintage Champagnes, the product of a single harvest, follow a similar pattern – lighter for *blanc de blancs*, richer for a blend of grape varieties. In general, however, they are richer, weightier and more honeyed than non-vintage Champagnes because they are aged for longer before they are released (*see* pages 102). This tends to make them (particularly if they are older vintages) more suitable for drinking with a meal.

Alternatives to Champagne

No place in France makes sparkling wine that quite matches the elegance of Champagne, though the so-called Crémant (Champagne method) wines, such as Crémant de Bourgogne and Crémant d'Alsace, make very acceptable alternatives. The two countries that succeed in coming closest to it are California and New Zealand – areas where the Champagne producers themselves have invested heavily. South Africa is another serious – though not always consistent – contender with its Méthode Cap Classique wines. But for an inexpensive Champagne substitute it's almost impossible to beat Spanish cava – a full-flavored yeasty sparkler that offers excellent value for the money.

If you find Champagne too dry, you may well find Australian sparkling wines more approachable. Generally made from Chardonnay, they offer smoother, creamier, fruitier drinking than their classic counterparts. Australia also produces some exuberantly fruity rosé sparkling wines and some wacky red sparklers. These come from grapes such as Shiraz, Grenache and Cabernet Sauvignon.

Tasting wheel

Wine: Blanc de
  Blancs Champagne
Dominant flavors:

apple

citrus

vanilla

cream

yeast

bread

biscuits

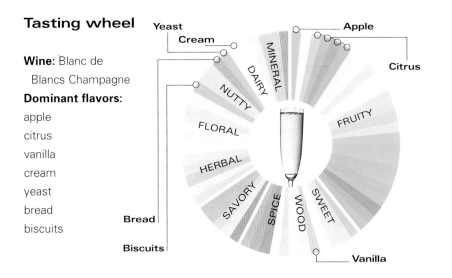

Other Champagne styles

Blanc de Blancs Champagne
Made entirely from Chardonnay
grapes, this style of Champagne
has a particularly elegant light,
creamy flavor.

Similar wines
New World (particularly Australian)
sparkling Chardonnays, and
some non-vintage Champagnes
such as Taittinger.

Vintage Champagne
Exactly which flavors you discover
does depend on how good the vintage
was and how old the bottle is, but a
six- to eight-year-old wine should be
rich, honeyed and toasty.

Similar wines
Nothing quite compares with vintage
Champagne. You'll find more
interesting variations between
vintages. Champagnes from 1990
(an outstanding year) for example, are
particularly rich, whereas those from
1991 and 1992 are much lighter in style.

Rosé Champagne

Despite its frivolous image, pink
Champagne is taken seriously in
France, with many producers offering
vintage versions. Younger wines tend to
be fresh and fruity, while older vintages
can acquire quite a mushroomy, truffley
character that makes them a
sophisticated accompaniment to classic
French cuisine. In Champagne they are
often served at formal dinners with red
meats such as lamb or even rare beef.

Tasting wheel

Wine: Vintage
  Champagne
Dominant flavors:

lemon

peach

grilled nuts

toast

honey

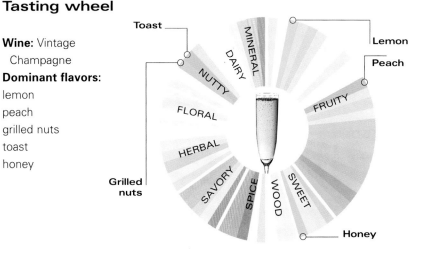

Similar wines
Australian pink sparklers tend to be
even fruitier. Try also inexpensive
strawberry-scented cava *rosados*.

Demi-sec (medium-dry) Champagne

An option if you find non-vintage
Champagne too dry, but most people
enjoy it more with cake or dessert.

Similar wines
Other French sparklers such as
Vouvray are made in a *demi-sec* or
moelleux style and go well with classic
French fruit tarts or flans. Alternatives
are the charmingly light, grapey,
Muscat-based sparklers from Italy –
wines such as Moscato d'Asti (better
quality than basic Asti), Prosecco
and the French Clairette de Die. Like
dessert wines, sweet sparkling wines
are hugely underrated, with many
people dismissing them, but the
combination of bubbles and sweetness
is, in fact, a perfect accompaniment
for lighter desserts such as mousses,
meringues, soufflés and fruit salads.

Enjoying wine

If I asked you to name the five most memorable wines you'd ever tasted, there probably wouldn't be much in common between them. They might include that quaffable white you drank on vacation (which never tasted the same when you got it home) or the first seductive top-red burgundy you ever drank. But I bet that in every instance the surroundings, the company and the mood you were in counted for more than the quality of the wine itself.

The lesson to draw from this is that wine doesn't have to be expensive to be enjoyable. You can get just as much pleasure from a simple country wine on a picnic as you do from an expensive Bordeaux. It's the occasion that counts.

Unfortunately, you can't guarantee these uniquely enjoyable experiences, but you can increase their likelihood. Thinking in terms of maximizing pleasure from your wine-drinking, rather than about how much (or little) you know about it is the key to really beginning to appreciate wine.

There are four things useful to remember and which I'll be covering over the next few pages:

- First, wine is seasonal. Take account of the temperature outside when you choose your bottle.
- Second, you can make people feel far more at ease by picking a wine they feel comfortable with. It just involves a bit of amateur psychology.
- Third, wine should be just as important a part of planning for major celebrations as the food and the venue. And it doesn't have to be expensive.
- And finally, the way you serve it also adds to the pleasure of the experience (*see* pages 46–7).

It's also worth learning a bit about the interplay between wine and food. Now that may sound like just one extra thing to worry about. But if you've ever tasted – as I'm sure you have – a perfect food and wine match, you'll know just how much pleasure that can give.

A lot of it is common sense. In fact it's a question of not trying to be too clever. If you're serving a French dish it's logical to serve the wine from the same region with it (the French wouldn't dream of doing anything else). If you cook a richly flavored spicy dish, serve a full-bodied wine alongside it rather than a light one.

And a lot of it is frankly trial and error. You can sometimes hit by accident on a winning combination just as you can transform a recipe by adding a single ingredient. So just as elsewhere in the book I've urged you to compare and contrast different wines (*see* pages 60–5 and 70–5), experiment with different combinations of food and wine, too. Serve two or more bottles and see which goes best and why you enjoy it more.

Wines for different seasons

Imagine a hot summer's day, warm enough to make you want to eat outdoors. Maybe you'll light a barbecue or simply throw together a simple salad. Nothing too heavy. Now imagine a winter evening with rain beating on the windows. Still going to serve that salad? Not on your life. That's the time for a big steaming bowl of soup or a rib-sticking stew.

It's second nature to adjust the kind of food you eat to the time of year, but how often do you do the same thing with wine? Yet, you no more want to drink a big gutsy red in the middle of a boiling hot day than a light, fruity rosé when there's snow on the ground. It's not so much that the wine doesn't taste right (big reds are in fact quite good with barbecued food), you're just not in the mood.

When it's hot or when you're tired, you want wines that are simple and refreshing. When it's cold, you want something more substantial and satisfying and you're often more mentally alert and prepared to make an effort to try something strange or unfamiliar.

Of course, given how unpredictable the weather can be, one can't make hard and fast rules about seasons. Spring sometimes comes ridiculously early, a summer's day can be gray and cloudy and autumn more like an Indian summer. Be led by the temperature outside, rather than the date on the calendar, but here are some broad guidelines to seasonal drinking that should give you some ideas.

Spring

At the first signs of spring you suddenly yearn for fresh, zesty flavors. Sauvignon Blanc fits the bill perfectly as do most crisp, inexpensive whites. If you're a Chardonnay lover, go for a lighter unoaked style. And move on to lighter, fruitier reds than those you've been drinking through the winter.

Summer

As the temperature climbs you frequently just want a glass of wine on its own. Good candidates are fragrant, aromatic whites such as Riesling, many of which are quite low in alcohol. In fact it's generally a good idea to stick to lighter wines – particularly around lunchtime. Follow the French habit of drinking rosé.

Autumn

With nights drawing in there's a "back to school" feel about autumn. Time to experiment with different grape varieties or discover a new country or region. If you're doing some formal entertaining take the opportunity to enjoy some of the more subtle, expressive wines, such as burgundy or a mature Rioja, after the simple fruit flavors of summer. They go well with seasonal foods such as mushrooms and game.

Winter

Comfort food. Comfort wine. That's what cold weather drinking should be about. Now's the time to enjoy those blockbuster reds and bring out those big oaky Chardonnays. And port isn't just for Christmas. Curl up in front of a blazing fire and treat yourself to a glass as a warming winter nightcap.

Christmas

Christmas is a time to play safe. With different generations gathering, you need bottles that are going to please everyone. You'll probably need six types of wine. A good quality, smooth, medium-bodied red and white for Christmas Day (France still impresses). An inexpensive fruity red and a white as a standby for impromptu parties and other family meals. Something indulgent, sweet and sticky (a half-bottle of dessert wine, or a bottle of port) and a bottle or two of bubbly (cava for parties, Champagne or a good-quality sparkling wine to celebrate Christmas or see in the New Year). Of course, exactly which wines you choose depends on what you are eating (*see* pages 34–9), but you won't go far wrong if you stick to the classics.

Outdoor eating

There's no point in buying expensive wines to eat out of doors – all that bracing fresh air kills subtle flavors stone dead. For picnics stick to crisp, dry whites, rosés, and soft fruity reds – not forgetting to chill the whites and rosés thoroughly before you go. (You can also buy insulated jackets to keep your bottles cool.) With all those spicy marinades barbecues present even more of a challenge. Super-fruity New World wines work best but steer clear of wines with too much oak or you'll end up with an overload of spice and smoke.

Wines for different people

Choosing wine, like planning a menu, is a question of psychology. Just as you wouldn't serve up a Thai green curry to your elderly aunt, you'd be unlikely to pour her a glass of Moroccan or Lebanese red. It's a question of horses for courses.

It's not difficult. It just needs a bit of forethought. If you're in doubt and it's an important occasion try the wine first – just as you'd try out a recipe you were preparing for the first time. And always have a bottle in reserve in case you find the wine is corked (*see* pages 50–1).

Here are some of the different types of guest you might have to deal with:

Wine experts
Genuine wine experts are easier to please than you'd imagine – so long as you don't make the mistake of buying the one wine they know a lot about (usually Bordeaux or burgundy). What they tend to enjoy are wines that are generally undervalued and unfashionable such as German and Alsace Riesling, sherry, Loire reds, and all kinds of dessert wine. But don't serve them if you don't enjoy them too.

Gourmets
With foodies it's how the wine goes with the meal that counts, so play to your culinary strengths. If you enjoy cooking Italian food learn about Italian wine. If you're good at curries, find out which wines go best with your favorite recipes (*see* pages 36–7). If desserts are your forte serve a sweet wine. (If they're not, serve stylish Vin Santo from Italy with *cantucci* dipping biscuits.)

Wine novices
People who don't know a lot about wine are often nervous about betraying their ignorance. Make life easy for them by serving wines you know they're likely to enjoy, such as unoaked Chardonnay and Merlot. This is not the time to reveal your lifelong love affair with mature German Riesling.

Wine snobs
The most tiresome people to deal with are those who are excessively impressed by names and labels. (Unlike the wine expert, they will regard any wine they haven't tasted before with deep suspicion.) The temptation is to make them look foolish by decanting a Romanian Pinot Noir and telling them it's a Nuits-St-Georges.

On the other hand, if it's the boss and you're working on a promotion, that might not be too clever. Well-known wines, such as Chablis and Châteauneuf-du-Pape always go down well with the label-conscious and are generally reliable.

Adventurous drinkers
Some friends just love to try anything that's different – from seafood laksa to Peruvian goat stew. There are plenty of quirky wines to match. Good hunting grounds are Portugal and southern Italy and wines from eccentric small producers (which you're more likely to find in an independent wine merchant). Serve several different bottles so they can mix and match.

Vegetarians and vegans
It's hospitable to take as much care with the wine you serve to your vegetarian friends as you do with the food. Vegetarian wines are wines on which no animal products have been used. Organic wines are produced without the aid of chemical sprays and fertilizers. Many wines meet both criteria; *see* pages 78–9.

One bottle or two?
How many different wines should you serve? If you serve a white wine before the meal you can carry it through the first course – then you can switch for the main course (you might like to offer a choice of white or red). And if it's a formal dinner you might want to serve a sweet dessert wine. Allow roughly two-thirds of a bottle (four glasses) a person, though it seems the more guests you have the less wine you tend to need.

Finally, don't worry too much. Remember, the vast majority of people don't mind what they drink as long as there's enough of it!

Right: The key to selecting wine for different people is to match the tone of the occasion. Make sure you have plenty of wine on hand and simply relax and enjoy!

Wines for different occasions

You might think there is an automatic answer to the question of which wine you should drink to celebrate the high points in life: Champagne. But there are other sparkling wines that might suit the occasion better – and which still make that celebratory pop.

The key thing to focus on with celebrations is the age group you're dealing with. Some occasions, such as weddings, tend to span the generations. Others, such as an 18th or 21st birthday or a golden wedding anniversary, involve predominantly one age group to whose tastes you might want to tailor the event.

Weddings

A family wedding is probably the most important occasion you're going to have to plan for, and the one at which you're most likely to want to serve Champagne. With large numbers to cater for price is likely to be the main consideration, but it's still important to find a Champagne you actually like. Even if a hotel or restaurant is doing the catering, they should be willing to let you sample the Champagne they propose to serve. And there's no reason why it has to be the same bottle all the way through. What people tend to remember is the first and last glass – so save a decent bottle for the toast.

18th or 21st birthdays

This is likely to be a predominantly young crowd, many of whom may not be used to wine. Although you may want to serve Champagne as a final toast, for the most part you could get away with an inexpensive sparkling wine (Australian sparkling wine is ideal as it's not too dry). Many of your guests may actually welcome some easy-drinking, fruity New World wines, not to mention a few beers. And remember to lay on plenty of water and soft drinks.

Christenings

Christenings are more often than not daytime events – and are most likely to be tea parties. If you're serving a lot of sweet things an ordinary Champagne will taste too dry. You're better off offering a *demi-sec* Champagne or – even better in my view – a glass of delicious, grapey Moscato d'Asti.

Golden wedding anniversaries and 70-plus birthdays

Unless your parents or grandparents happen to be French or Italian, they may be of a generation where wine drinking is not so much the norm, so stick to wine they're familiar with, or that you know they'll like. Older people tend to develop a taste for softer, slightly sweeter wines, so consider medium-dry whites and mature oak-aged reds such as Rioja. And they're more likely than most groups to appreciate a vintage Champagne or a special bottle you've been keeping for the occasion.

Left and right: Champagne may seem the obvious choice for most special occasions, but, in fact, sparkling wines can be just as suitable.

Valentine's Day, anniversaries and other romantic occasions

Intimate dinners have the advantage that there's only two of you to consider, so the key is to take into account your partner's tastes. (After all, there's no point in serving Champagne if they don't like it.) Resist the temptation to ply him or her with a lot of expensive wine. He or she may simply fall asleep!

Other parties

Parties tend to be hot and crowded so it's better to choose wines that are light and fruity rather than too heavy or oaky. Many people dislike wines that are too sharp, so avoid ultra-dry whites or very cheap reds. Remember, unalleviated sparkling wine can be quite acidic, so it's always worth having some still wines at hand. And allow half a bottle, in total, per person.

Matching food and wine

Choosing a wine to go with a meal used to be relatively easy. You drank white with fish and red with meat and that was that. But now that the range of wines available is so vast and we're exposed to so many different and exotic kinds of food, life is a lot more complicated.

A lot of people say it doesn't matter and you should drink what you like – which is fine if you're eating on your own. But if you're entertaining, you have to take into account other people's tastes and there aren't too many who enjoy medium-dry white wine with steak.

Two of the old rules that still make a lot of sense are to serve lighter wines before full-bodied ones and drier wines before sweeter – just as you wouldn't dream of starting a dinner party with dessert. But, more important than the old white-with-fish and red-with-meat rule is the style of the food you're serving.

Ask yourself what is the most important influence on the dish – whether it's based on meat, fish or vegetables. Is it the flavoring ingredients or the way it's cooked? To take fish as an example, if it was curried or cooked in a garlicky *provençal* sauce, the most important factor would be the origin of the dish and the flavor of seasoning ingredients (consult the following pages to see which wines work best with different cuisines).

If, on the other hand, your fish was grilled or fried, the cooking method might be the more important influence. While you probably wouldn't, for instance, want to serve a fruity red wine with a seafood salad, it would be great with a piece of pan-seared salmon. You need to think about the overall weight of the dish, and pick your wine to match. Is it a light and fresh dish or is it rich and heavy?

If you find it difficult at first, as I did, just think of wine as adding an extra ingredient, as you would when you're cooking. When you cook fried fish you often add a squeeze of lemon. Well, a crisp, citrussy white works in exactly the same way.

The logic behind chocolate and sweet red wine, for example, makes sense when you think of the classic chocolate and cherry combination of Black Forest Gâteau. Look at the fruit flavors on the flavor wheel and imagine how they'd work with the dish you're planning to serve.

You can also affect the way a wine tastes by the food you pair it with. Oaky wines, for example, taste less oaky when you drink them with roast or grilled meat (particularly if it's slightly underdone). Slightly sharp whites taste less tart with acidic foods such as tomato or salads. Sweet wines can taste almost dry if you partner them with a very sweet dessert (which is why your wine should be sweeter than your pudding).

Wine also affects the taste of food. Wines with a high level of acidity – crisp whites or light, fruity reds – can cut through rich or slightly fatty foods such as *pâté* or rich pasta dishes, making them seem less heavy.

The other important thing to remember is that the more that's going on on the plate, the bolder your wines need to be to stand up to it. So, if you're serving a particularly fine wine and want to do it justice, keep the food as simple and unfussy as possible.

Top left
Roast Dover sole with wild mushrooms.
Although the fish appears plainly cooked, the fact that it is accompanied by richly flavored wild mushrooms suggests a full-bodied rather than a light, crisp dry white. A Meursault or a California Chardonnay would be ideal.

Top right
Red wine ragout of fish.
Here, fish is given a much more robust treatment than usual, served almost like a *coq au vin* with a richly flavored red wine sauce. The dish could handle an equally robust red wine such as a Gigondas or Crozes-Hermitage.

Bottom left
Fruits de mer en croustade.
A classic French fish dish with a rich buttery sauce. It isn't quite as strongly flavored as the mushroom dish, but you do need at least a medium-bodied wine to handle the richness. A white burgundy such as St-Véran would work well.

Bottom right
Fritto misto mare.
The fact that the fish is fried should dictate your choice. What you need is a wine that will act like a squeeze of lemon, counteracting any greasiness. Any crisp dry white would do, but as the dish is Italian, go for a Frascati or Pinot Grigio.

Wine-loving countries

In much of Europe wine drinking is a way of life. The local wine is enjoyed alongside the local food and there's no great desire to explore what is unfamiliar. A Frenchman in the Rhône would no more think of drinking a Muscadet from the Loire than he would an Australian Chardonnay. There's no reason why you should follow suit, but you may well find that the tried and tested combinations are hard to improve upon.

France

Although French cooking is a byword for *haute cuisine*, the food the French themselves most enjoy is quite rustic, and specific to their region. In areas where there is seafood (the Loire and southern France) there are plenty of crisp, dry whites to go with it.

In inland areas such as Burgundy the more robust meat dishes of the region, such as *coq au vin* and *boeuf bourguignonne*, are cooked in and accompanied by the local wine. In Alsace the creaminess of the sauces finds an echo in the rich spiciness of a Riesling or Pinot Gris. In France everywhere there is *charcuterie*, there is a simple fresh red or white to wash it down.

In the south of France the cooking is dominated by the vivid Mediterranean flavors of tomato, garlic, olives and anchovies, all quite pungent and challenging to wine. Crisp, dry, earthy whites and rosés* handle them best – and reflect the "summery" mood of the region. More robust dishes respond to spicy reds based on Syrah and Grenache, the kind you generally find in the Rhône and the Languedoc.

These wines are also good solutions for other Mediterranean cuisines such as those from Greece, Slovenia and Croatia.

Italy

Who doesn't eat pizza or pasta? Italian food is so well loved, and so internationalized, that one tends to forget it's regional too. When in Italy, drink the local wine. Otherwise Italian wines in general are wonderfully food-friendly and flexible. Neutral Italian whites such as Pinot Grigio, Orvieto and Soave work with a wide range of *antipasti*, risottos and pastas such as *spaghetti carbonara*, with seafood salads, squid or *fritto misto mare*, with *scallopine* and *osso buco*. In fact, about the only thing that defeats them is richly sauced meat or game (with which you need something like an Amarone or a Barolo). Fruity, slightly sharp Italian reds such as Barbera, Chianti and Valpolicella are equally good with pizza and richer pasta dishes, as well as the grilled and roasted meat dishes Italians love.

Spain and Portugal

The Moorish influence is quite noticeable in Spanish food. Flavors such as saffron, garlic, pimento and chili make it spicier than you might expect. Dry whites, *rosados* (rosé) and, in the south, fino sherry, all go well with these ingredients and with seafood dishes such as *paella*. The superb grilled lamb you find throughout northern Spain is a perfect foil for its famous oak-aged reds such as Rioja and Ribera del Duero. Portugal shares a broadly similar cuisine, but with more emphasis on seafood. Dry whites, such as the local Vinho Verde, serve well.

Germany, Austria and Switzerland

German food is almost as poorly known outside Germany as many of its best wines, but the unique combination of sweetness and acidity in its most famous grape, Riesling, suits the cuisine to perfection. Crisp Kabinetts can handle a wide range of dishes, from creamily sauced trout to *sauerkraut* to the smoked sausages and robust pork dishes that are so popular with the locals, while slightly sweeter Spätlese Rieslings are brilliant with duck and goose. And Germany's growing number of serious reds can tackle more robust game dishes such as venison.

Austria comes under a more central European influence with the spicy, paprika-seasoned foods finding an echo in peppery reds such as Blaufränkisch. Switzerland reflects the food of its two main cultural influences, France and Germany, but the custom of drinking dry whites such as Chasselas with Switzerland's many cheese-based dishes underlines the fact that white wine can be just as successful as red with cheese.

Left: The classic Mediterranean flavors of olives, tomatoes, garlic and chili are perfectly matched by southern French, Italian and Spanish wines.

Spicy, Oriental and fusion food

Unlike the wine-producing countries of Europe, the newer wine-producing countries and regions of Australia, California, New Zealand and South Africa do not have the same kind of deep rooted traditional cuisine of their own – instead they borrow from every other cuisine that excites their imagination. (It's true now of Britain too.) On the other hand, you have countries with a wonderful culinary heritage, such as China and Thailand, who have no wine industry to speak of and where there are no established food and wine matches. With no precedents to constrain you, you can have a lot of fun experimenting with different combinations. Here are some starting points you might find useful.

Middle Eastern and North African

The food of the southern Mediterranean is spicier than that of the north. Spices such as cumin and coriander are common to the cuisines of Turkey, Egypt and Lebanon, while in Morocco they're joined by saffron and chilli. The best wine choices tend to be simple, inexpensive dry whites, reds and rosés, and for fuller-flavored dishes such as *tagines*, more robust, rustic reds – the kind you find in Morocco.

Indian

There's a myth that wine doesn't go with Indian food. Well I wouldn't put my best bottle of burgundy with it, but there's no reason why you shouldn't drink wine with curry if you enjoy it. The thing to remember is that there are many different styles of Indian food, with differing degrees of spiciness.

For milder Indian dishes I generally find that simple, crisp whites and rosés work best. With hotter dishes I prefer a ripe, fruity white such as a Sémillon or a sweet, jammy Australian or Chilean red.

Chinese

One of the great cuisines of the world – and, again, very varied. Most people's perception of Chinese food is based on the more delicate, refined flavors of Cantonese food, though some dishes (such as Szechuan) are hotter. German Kabinett Riesling and Alsace Gewurztraminer most frequently recommended wines because they have a useful touch of sweetness, but any off-dry white (such as an Australian Colombard) should do. Light, fruity reds work better than oak-aged reds.

Japanese

Not the easiest of cuisines to tackle (the Japanese traditionally drink sake), but it is increasingly fashionable, and so it's worth considering which wines to serve with it. With raw fish such as *sushi*, *sashimi*, or *tempura*, try a bone-dry white such as Muscadet or (if you're feeling extravagant) a *blanc de blancs* Champagne. With spicier dishes such as *teriyaki*, try a light, fruity red such as Beaujolais.

Thai

Although Thai food is hot, the main seasoning ingredients – coriander, ginger, lime leaves and lemongrass – are surprisingly wine-friendly. I'd go for any crisp, citrussy New World white – New Zealand Sauvignon Blanc would be perfect. You could also try an Australian or New Zealand Riesling or Verdelho. Satay is tricky – try an Australian Chardonnay.

Central and Southwest American

Chilis are the common factor here. You can't beat big, sweet, jammy reds such as Zinfandel or Chilean and Californian Cabernet Sauvignon, though, if the dish is really hot, watch out for flavor overload. (A more restrained alternative is a young Rioja, which is surprisingly good.) Sauvignon Blanc copes well with the raw tomato, lime and coriander combination you frequently find in Mexican cooking.

Fusion food

Increasingly, modern international menus feature one or more of these cuisines. Either choose a wine that goes with a wide range of flavors (*see* restaurants, pages 40–1) or try the recommendations I have outlined above.

Right: Exotic Eastern flavors find exciting partners in the bold, flavorsome wines of the New World. Riesling and Sauvignon work particularly well.

Combinations that work

Here's a brief checklist of tried-and-true combinations that generally work well.

Meat
• Light meats, such as chicken, turkey, pork and veal, generally take on the character of other ingredients. Plainly cooked, they go equally well with light- or medium-bodied reds or whites.
• Grilled and roast beef and lamb suit most kinds of medium- or full-bodied reds. Quickly sautéed meat, such as calf's liver, is better suited to lighter reds.
• The stronger flavors of game suit Pinot Noir and mature, oak-aged reds such as Rioja. Duck and goose, being a little fattier, often go well with Riesling.
• For rich, dark braises such as oxtail, venison and hare, try robust, full-bodied reds such as Barolo and Zinfandel.
• Cold meats and *charcuterie* suit simple, fruity reds and crisp, dry whites.

Fish
• Raw shellfish is perfect with crisp, dry whites such as Muscadet (oysters and Chablis is a classic combination).
• Cooked shellfish, such as lobster, langoustines and scallops, deserve a good burgundy or any other top-quality Chardonnay, or even Champagne.
• Plainly cooked fish: crisp or smooth dry whites – not too fruity or heavily oaked. Fine fish, such as sole, salmon and turbot, will show off the best whites.
• Oily fish such as sardines, mackerel or whitebait: a crisp, lemony white. Meaty fish such as salmon and tuna – ideal for grilling – can take a light red.

• Smoked fish: Try German Kabinett Riesling or a fino sherry. Smoked salmon goes well with Champagne, Riesling or Sauvignon Blanc.

Eggs
Breakfast/brunch style dishes such as scrambled eggs and omelettes: a light Chardonnay or Champagne (or a sparkling wine equivalent). These wines also suit quîche and egg-based sauces such as hollandaise and mayonnaise. Béarnaise is often better with a light red.

Cheese
Not always the marriage made in heaven you might imagine – particularly where extremely ripe cheeses are concerned. With soft, unrinded and washed-rind cheeses, white is often better than red (fresh goat cheese and Sauvignon Blanc is a great combination). If you're serving cheese to finish off a red you've been drinking with the main course, go for a hard cheese such as Cheddar, Gouda – or, even better with a fine wine – Parmesan. While not to everyone's taste, blue cheese works surprisingly well with sweet wines. (Roquefort with Sauternes and Stilton with Port are the two classic combinations.) The best advice if you value your wine is not to overload your cheeseboard with too many different kinds of cheese.

Vegetables
Uncooked or lightly cooked vegetables and salads: crisp whites and dry rosés. More robust vegetable dishes based on mushrooms or aubergines can often take an equally robust red. Tricky candidates are asparagus (Sauvignon or unoaked Chardonnay), tomatoes (inexpensive white or rosé) and artichokes (no perfect solution but how often do you eat artichokes?).

Desserts
• If you have a sweet wine you want to show off, the best option is simple, French fruit tarts (apples, pears peaches and apricots are more flattering than sharper red fruits such as strawberries and raspberries, though a little *crème patissière* helps).
• Light-textured mousses, meringues and soufflés can be good with a semi-sweet sparkling wine such as Moscato d'Asti or a *demi-sec* Champagne. (Moscato also works well with fruit salad and lemon-flavored desserts.)
• *Crème brûlée* is a good friend to dessert wine, but chocolate can be difficult. Try an Australian Orange Muscat, a sweet red wine, or a ruby or late-bottled vintage port. And for ultra-sweet desserts such as sticky toffee pudding and pecan pie? It's hard to beat Liqueur Muscat.

Tricky ingredients and seasonings
The following are all likely to do terrible things to wine. Avoid them if you can: Foods that are very acidic (lemon juice, vinegar, sharp salad dressings and sour pickles); very hot (habanero chilis) or very cold (ice cream and sorbets). Kippers and bloaters (far better with tea). Raw onion.

Eating out – choosing wine in a restaurant

Few people, if the truth be told, actually enjoy being handed the wine list. The responsibility for choosing a wine that everyone is going to enjoy, let alone one that will go with what they are eating, is a heavy one. Yet, they often hesitate to ask for advice for fear of appearing ignorant.

The dilemma is easily resolved if you go to one of the growing number of restaurants that offer a good selection of wines by the glass. Although it generally costs a bit more than ordering wine by the bottle, it means that everyone can pick exactly what they prefer, just as they can with food. But what if you are faced with a lengthy and unfamiliar wine list? Here are some tips that may help.

• If you are in a restaurant, in a wine-producing area, it's always best to choose a local wine.

• In theory, the house wine should be a decent value but, in practice, the quality generally relates to the overall standard and choice on the list.

A selection of three or four recommended wines should indicate a more thoughtful approach, but do make sure there aren't better bargains in the main body of the list.

• Don't be afraid to ask for a recommendation, even in a smart restaurant. Sommeliers like the chance to show off their food and wine matching skills. Try to give an indication of the price you are prepared to pay, so that you aren't put in the embarrassing situation of having a wine suggested that costs more than you can afford – simply point to a similar wine and say "I was wondering about that."

• If your waiter doesn't appear to know much about wine, play safe with wines you know. Flexible wines that work with a wide range of dishes are Italian whites such as Pinot Grigio, unoaked Chardonnay, New World Sauvignon; also Pinot Noir and Merlot. Australian wines rarely let you down.

• Restaurants put higher mark-ups on wines from areas such as Bordeaux and Burgundy than on lesser-known wines, which can be good bargains. Examples of such bargains include wines from Alsace and from up-and-coming areas of the Languedoc, such as Pic St-Loup. If your waiter recommends something unfamiliar, be prepared to give it a try.

• Watch out for and avoid vintages that have passed their sell-by-date – particularly in the case of inexpensive whites (*see* page 44).

What to do if the wine is faulty

Your waiter should show you the bottle before opening it so that you can confirm it's what you ordered (check the vintage and producer). When he or she hands you the glass, swirl the wine around and take a sniff. You should be able to tell if there's something wrong with it without even having to taste it (*see* pages 52–3). If it's cloudy or smells musty or unpleasant, reject it immediately. It should be replaced without question.

If it smells okay, take a sip. Even if the wine is not faulty you have a right to expect that it should be pleasant to drink. If it's sharp or vinegary, again send it back. If it's simply not what you were expecting you're on trickier ground. If it's a wine you're unfamiliar with and you simply don't like it, you have no real right to complain, but a restaurant that values your patronage may be willing to change it.

It's also reasonable to expect the wine to be served at the right temperature. If it's too warm ask for it to be chilled a little longer. If it's too cold make sure the bottle isn't put straight back in the ice bucket. And there's no reason why you shouldn't ask for a fruity red to be lightly chilled – particularly during the summer.

Buying wine

O ne shouldn't really complain, but these days there are almost too many ways to buy wine and too many bottles to choose from. With some supermarkets stocking 600–700 different wines, it's not surprising that many people fall back on the ones they already know. If you want to avoid impulse buys you might regret, it's worth weighing up what the various outlets have to offer.

Above and right: Despite the romance of buying wine direct from the producer, most of us buy wine from shops, whether they be supermarkets or specialty merchants.

Supermarkets vs specialist wine shops

Reasonable prices and the convenience of being able to buy a bottle with your groceries means supermarkets are where most people buy their wines for everyday drinking. But if you need advice or want something a little out of the ordinary, you're better off with a specialist. Some independent shops also have bottles open for tasting so you can try before you buy.

Mail order and the net

Buying by mail order – or the internet – is attractive, probably because you don't have to haul all those bottles home. And it's fun browsing through websites and merchants' wine lists, many of which feature interesting stories about the wines they sell. Watch out, though, for pre-selected cases that may contain wines that haven't sold well and are nearing the end of their shelf life. And be wary of advertisements in newspapers offering top wines such as Bordeaux and Champagne at unusually cheap prices.

Buying direct

If you're lucky enough to live near, or be vacationing in, a wine-producing region, buying direct from the cellar door can be a lot of fun – though it isn't always cheaper than buying from a shop. It can also be tricky to handle if you don't like any of the wines – particularly if you've got the wine-maker standing at the other side of the counter. But steel yourself and make your apologies. There's no point in buying wine you don't like.

Auctions

Not for novices. You need to know your producers and your vintages and be able to assess the condition of the wines you're going to buy. Go along and enjoy yourself but leave the bidding to the experts.

Investing in wine

It's undoubtedly true that you can make money in wine just as you can with stocks and shares, but it's a gamble unless you've got money to burn on classics that hold their value. The best policy is to only buy wines you would actually enjoy drinking if the bottom fell out of the market. Some wines you have to buy *en primeur* (i.e. before they're released) if you're to have a chance of getting hold of them at all – or at least buying them at an affordable price. If you do put your money upfront, make sure you're dealing with a reputable company.

Buying tips

• Inexpensive wines – particularly whites and rosés – aren't intended to be kept for more than a few months. Buy from the current vintage.

• Bin ends are basically stock the shopkeeper or mail order company wants to clear. They're only a bargain if you intend to drink them right away.

• Wines that have been standing upright or under a hot spotlight may not be in the best condition. Watch out for bottles that are sticky or seeping under the foil cap.

• If a wine is faulty (*see* pages 50–1), advise the company you bought it from immediately.

• Remember, half-bottles age more quickly and should therefore be drunk sooner than standard bottles. Magnums (double-sized bottles) mature more slowly.

• Unsplit cases (i.e. all the same wine) are almost always cheaper than mixed cases, but be sure you like the wine enough to buy that much of it.

Storing and serving wine

You might think that once you've picked your bottle of wine that's it. You've done the hard part. But, surprisingly, how you treat your wine once you get it home – and in particular how you store it – can make a big difference to the way it tastes.

Left: A modern wine rack, such as this, may be decorative but is only suitable for keeping wine in the short-term.

Storing wine

If you intend to keep your wine for any length of time you have to pick your spot. The conditions in a traditional wine cellar – cool, dark and damp – are perfect, but some people don't have cellars.

Wine doesn't do well in extremes of temperature, so don't leave it in places like a garage, where temperatures can swing wildly between freezing and stiflingly hot. Similarly, don't keep wine next to a furnace or on top of the fridge. The best kind of place is a cool, dark cupboard where the wine can remain quietly undisturbed. But make sure you don't store strong-smelling things such as cleaning products there too.

The key thing to remember is to store your bottles horizontally. That keeps the cork moist and ensures air – the great enemy of wine – doesn't seep into the bottle.

How long does wine keep?

The biggest mistake people make is to keep wine for too long. Most modern wine is designed to be drunk immediately. Obviously, if you buy a bottle just after it's been released, it will last for longer than if it's been on the shelf for several months but, as a general rule, drink inexpensive whites and rosés within three months, light reds and slightly more expensive whites, such as Chardonnay, within six, and most other inexpensive reds within a year. That's not to say they won't still be perfectly drinkable if you leave them for longer, but their character may well change (*see* pages 86–7).

Serving

There's a lot of mystique about serving wine, but in truth there are only four things you need to remember – all of which will add to your enjoyment:

Serve it at the right temperature

The mistake most people make is to serve white wine too cold and reds too warm. If you leave a bottle of wine in the fridge for several hours it kills the wine's more subtle flavors. Depending on the efficiency of your fridge, 45 minutes to an hour is enough for a full-bodied white such as a Chardonnay, and up to an hour and a half for crisp, dry whites, aromatic wines such as Riesling, and sweet and sparkling wines. Lighter reds, such as Beaujolais and Pinot Noir, also benefit from being lightly chilled, but even more full-bodied reds shouldn't be allowed to get too warm and soupy – don't leave them next to a radiator or in the full sun.

If you forget to chill a wine or need to chill it at the last minute, either plunge the bottle into a bucket of iced water or pop it briefly (15 minutes maximum) in the freezer. You can also buy insulated jackets to freeze and then slip over the bottle.

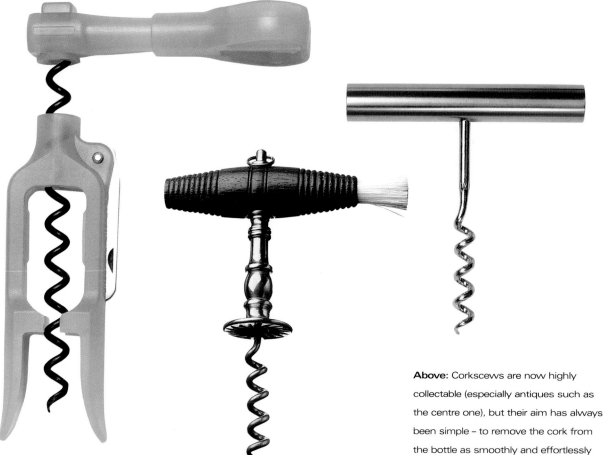

Above: Corkscews are now highly collectable (especially antiques such as the centre one), but their aim has always been simple – to remove the cork from the bottle as smoothly and effortlessly as possible. The "Screwpull", on the far left, is the most practical.

Get a decent corkscrew

Opening a bottle of wine can be a struggle, so it's worth investing in a corkscrew that will do the hard work for you. The simplest, most inexpensive type is the so-called "waiter's friend," but I think it is worth paying a little more for one that's simpler to use. It's also worth having one with a foil cutter so you can easily remove the cap.

With Champagne bottles and other sparkling wines, opening the bottle is simply a matter of practice. Remove the foil and the wire that holds the cork in place. Holding on to the cork with your left hand, twist the base of the bottle with your right (reverse this if you are left handed) and you should feel the cork begin to ease out. Just hold on to the cork and let the pressure inside the bottle do the work for you – there's no need for an explosive pop. Have your glasses at hand and hold them at an angle to the bottle as you pour (just as you would a beer) so that the bubbles don't cascade over the side of the glass. And remember, Champagne should always be well chilled before you attempt to open it.

Buy generously sized wine glasses

It's better to buy glasses that are practical rather than decorative (some, of course, are both). The ideal wine glass is clear (so you can see the color

of the wine), with a long stem so you don't have to grasp it around the top, a generously sized bowl tapering slightly towards the rim (to trap the aromas), and a fine, thin rim that helps you to sip the wine, rather than gulp it down. When you pour you should only fill the glass to between half and two-thirds up so you can swirl the wine around (*see* pages 52–3) without pouring it over yourself. (Always check, when you pour the first glass, that the wine isn't corked; *see* pages 50–1.)

You may, if you're enthusiastic about wine, want to buy more than one type of glass. The two extra ones that would top my list are a tall, narrow Champagne flute (better than a wine glass for preserving the bubbles) and a smaller glass for dessert or fortified wines. If you like to serve different wines during the meal you might also want a second set of wine glasses. It's traditional to choose a slightly smaller glass for white than for red, but it doesn't matter hugely.

Finally – obvious but crucial – keep your glasses scrupulously clean and grease free. And don't store them upside down as it traps stale air inside the glass.

Decanting is just another word for pouring

Contrary to what most people believe, you don't get a lot of benefit from just pulling the cork. It is exposing wine to air that makes a difference. You really only need to decant wine when it has a sediment you want to get rid of (which only tends to happen with older, unfiltered reds or vintage port), or if it is particularly full-bodied and needs to soften up a bit.

To decant a wine, leave the bottle upright for at least 24 hours, then, with a light behind the neck of the bottle (a candle or an up-ended flame will do), pour steadily and carefully until you see the sediment edging towards the mouth of the bottle. Then stop. You don't have to have a decanter – you can use an ordinary pitcher or carafe.

In general, you should decant a wine about one to two hours before serving it, except in the case of very old wines whose fragile aromas and flavors can easily evaporate on exposure to the air.

Storing wine once the bottle is open

If you have any wine left over you can store it for a couple of days in the fridge; if you can transfer it to a smaller bottle, so much the better. Curiously, I've noticed that traditionally made (particularly French) wines survive better than very fruity New World wines which often lose their impact if left open for more than a few hours. French wines are even better the day after opening.

You can buy wine preservation systems that pump the air out of the bottle, or protect the wine with an inert gas, but they shouldn't encourage you to keep it for days (or more than a week in the case of sweet wines).

Fortified wines such as port will keep longer, but even they shouldn't be kept for more than a month. Dry sherries should be treated like white wine and drunk within a couple of days, which is why it makes sense to buy them in half-bottles (*see* page 115).

Above: The "Vacuvin" pump is ideal for storing a bottle of wine once opened for a couple of days.
Left: Decanting a wine exposes it to the air but is rarely necessary for modern wines.

Wine and health

The big boom in the sales of red wine owes a lot to the increasing acceptance that moderate drinking helps to protect against heart disease. Although some authorities claim this benefit for any kind of alcohol, a sizeable body of scientific opinion holds that it is the phenolic compounds in the skins of red grapes that offer the greatest protection. In evidence they point to the so-called French Paradox – the fact that the wine-loving French consume a diet that is rich in animal and dairy fat, yet have a surprisingly low rate of heart disease.

Before you rush off to crack open a bottle, the key to all the health studies is moderation. Officially recommended limits are still quite modest.

To work out whether you are keeping within sensible limits, you need to check the alcohol content of the wine you're drinking – expressed on the label as percentage ABV (alcohol by volume). A small glass of Mosel Kabinett Riesling at eight percent, for instance, would only be one unit. A beefy 14-percent Australian Shiraz would be 1.8. (If you want to work out how many units there are in a particular wine, multiply the volume in millilitres by the percent ABV and divide by 1000. For example, a 13-percent Chardonnay would work out as 750ml x 13 divided by 1000 = 9.75 units per bottle: in other words. approximately 1.6 units a glass.)

If this sounds like too much maths, the basic thing to remember is that some wines are much more alcoholic than others. You may think, if you're drinking a white wine such as Chardonnay, that you're well within the limit, but it's incredibly easy to clock up those units. Most official calculations are based on small wine glasses – the generously sized glasses, used in many restaurants, now can contain far more wine than you think.

Possible adverse effects

Apart from the obvious symptoms that result from drinking too much (*see* below), some people also react

Left: In wine-loving Mediterranean countries, heart disease is surprisingly low.

adversely to certain types of wines. The most common culprit, especially in inexpensive whites, is sulphur, to which some people (particularly asthmatics) are quite sensitive. Other people find that the histamines in reds give them headaches. If you have problems of this kind it's worth trying organic wines, which avoid the use of sprays and additives, and keep sulphur to a minimum (*see* pages 78–9).

Wine and weight

It doesn't look as if it does, but unfortunately wine contains calories – quite a lot of them, in fact. And white is no better than red. If you're watching your weight, you're better off choosing a wine that's 12 percent alcohol or less. A dry, crisp white or light Italian red will set you back around 90 calories – 30 calories less than a rich, barrel-fermented Chardonnay or an Australian Shiraz. Bone-dry fino or manzanilla sherry at around 80 calories a glass is also a good bet. But avoid port and sweet sherry, which may contain up to 135 calories in a small glass.

Low-alcohol options

Apart from low-alcohol wine (which doesn't really deserve to be regarded as wine at all), if you don't want to drink too much, there are ways of diluting the alcohol content of the wines you enjoy. One of the most palatable is a spritzer – a half-and-half mixture of white wine and soda. Another is Mimosa, a mix of Champagne or sparkling wine and orange juice. Italian sparkling wines, such as Moscato d'Asti, are also naturally low in alcohol.

Tips for safe drinking

• Avoid drinking wine on an empty stomach.
• Don't drink alcohol because you're thirsty. Have a glass of water or other soft drink before you have your first glass of wine, and ideally in-between glasses too.
• At parties take care that your glass isn't being refilled without you realizing it.
• It's better to drink a moderate amount regularly than an excessive amount occasionally. You can't save your alcohol-free days up to have a binge.
• Don't drink alcohol and drive.

Hangovers

Okay, so you didn't take all this good advice and you've got a hangover. What's the best way to get rid of it? Although there are people who swear by a prairie oyster (a repulsive morning-after cocktail of Worcestershire sauce, tomato ketchup and egg yolk, heavily seasoned with pepper), I advocate the simple remedy of water, vitamin C and paracetamol. Take a couple of paracetamol and drink as much water as you can before going to bed, then repeat the dose if necessary in the morning. Alcohol also affects the body's ability to absorb vitamin C, so treat yourself to a large glass of freshly squeezed orange juice.

Alcohol units/alcohol level

Check the level of alcohol on the label against this list for the units per glass.

Wine

% vol	units per glass (125 ml)
15.0	1.9
14.5	1.8
14.0	1.8
13.5	1.7
13.0	1.6
12.5	1.6
12.0	1.5
11.5	1.4
11.0	1.4
10.5	1.3
10.0	1.3
9.5	1.2
9.0	1.1
8.5	1.1
8.0	1.0
7.5	0.9
7.0	0.9

Sherry

% vol	units per measure (50ml)
18.0	0.9
17.5	0.9

Port

% vol	units per measure (50ml)
22.0	1.1
21.5	1.1
21.0	1.1
20.0	1.0

Figures provided by the Health Education Authority.

How to tell if something is wrong with your wine

If you're a relatively inexperienced wine-drinker it's sometimes difficult to tell whether the flavors you find unpalatable are genuine faults, or a matter of personal taste. Sometimes a wine is so disgusting that it's obvious there's something wrong with it, but on other occasions it's harder to feel confident about your reaction.

Basically, however, it comes down to common sense. Even if you buy a cheap bottle of wine you've a right to expect that it should be clean, fresh and fruity. If it isn't, it might simply be over the hill – but that isn't acceptable. And it certainly shouldn't be sour, bitter, cloudy or fizzy (unless it's a sparkling wine).

It's more difficult when you simply find the flavors in your glass rather odd, a situation you often get with older wines. The petrolly smell of mature Riesling, the farm-yardy, agricultural smell of old burgundy, and the rank, sour aromas and flavors you can get from Sauvignon Blanc, are all considered by the trade to be within the bounds of acceptability, but may seem quite unpleasant to you. Unfortunately, there's not a lot you can do if you don't like them – except stick to younger wines.

Above: Oxidized wine has a brownish yellow color, almost like sherry.

What wine should look like

Still wines should be clear and bright. If they're not, there's almost certainly some kind of problem with the wine, or air has got into the bottle through the cork. Whites in particular should never be brown in color (although older reds may fade to a brickish red). Do not worry if you find small crystals in the bottom of your glass – they're quite harmless.

Corkiness and other wine faults

Most wine problems stem from the bottle being corked, which doesn't mean – as many people think – it has bits of cork floating in it, but that the wine has become contaminated by a defective cork. The effect is usually quite obvious, with the wine smelling positively moldy, but it

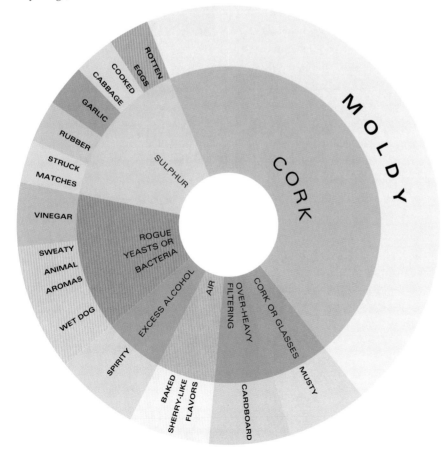

can simply dull the flavors and aromas of the wine. If a wine smells musty, the reason may also lie in the glasses being dirty, or having been left upside down in a cupboard, trapping in stale air.

Other common problems are generally winemaking faults. Many aromas, such as a rotten-egg, cooked-cabbage, hot-rubber or a struck-match smell, relate to the use of sulphur by the winemaker. Others, such as vinegary, cheesy, animal or sweaty aromas, are generally the result of rogue bacteria or yeasts having got into the winemaking process. They tend to be more common (and are sometimes even considered desirable) in traditional winemaking areas, such as Burgundy, Rhône, southwest France, the Loire, and parts of Spain and Italy, than in New World countries where winemakers are fanatical about cleanliness and hygiene.

Unpleasant flavors you might find in wine

On the far left is a "bad" flavor wheel that illustrates the more unpleasant aromas and flavors. Sometimes they dissipate in the glass, or when you leave the bottle open. You can also try to get rid of them by pouring the wine into a container and swirling it around. If they persist, however, the wine is almost certainly faulty. If in doubt, don't hesitate to take, or send, the bottle back.

Alternatives to cork

Given that anything between one in ten and one in twenty bottles is believed to be corked, it would save a lot of problems if there were alternative ways to stopper bottles. In fact, the technology exists in the form of sophisticated synthetic corks and even screwcaps, but most winemakers claim that customers are resistant to them. Apart from the one difficulty of removing synthetic corks off your corkscrew, they're more efficient in every respect. But in the end, the choice is up to you. Be prepared to buy your wine with a synthetic cork or screwcap, or put up with the regular risk of a faulty bottle.

Tasting wine

One of the most offputting things about wine is watching a professional taste. All that sniffing, noisy sucking in of air and spitting … is it really necessary and do you have to follow suit?

Pretentious as it may seem, what the expert is doing is quite practical. He or she sniffs because smell is 90 percent of taste (just think how little you can taste when you have a cold). The slurping noise is to draw air in through the mouth to release the flavor of the wine. And spitting is simply to make sure he doesn't end up horizontal – but then he's probably tasting 100 bottles, rather than the three or four you might have in front of you.

However, it is worth learning how to taste properly because it will increase your enjoyment of wine. If you sniff as well as sip you get double the pleasure – you can enjoy the wine's fabulous (or at least I hope they're fabulous) aromas and then have the pleasure of rolling it around in your mouth.

Don't be put off if you're not discovering the flavors you expect in a wine or those other people around you seem to find. What aromas or flavors you recognize depend on whether, or how often, you've encountered them before. Check your impressions against the flavors on the flavor wheel (*see* page 9). If you're not used to describing wine – or hearing it described – you may also find the flavor crib on pages 136–7 and the list of tasting terms on pages 138–9 helpful. This is how to do it:

Step one

Fill your glass about a quarter full – no more than this or the wine will slop over the sides when you swirl it. (Even when you pour wine to drink for pleasure, it's better not to overfill your glass or you'll find it hard to release the wine's aromas – *see* step three.)

Step two

Tilt your glass and look at the color (it helps to have a light background behind the glass). The most important thing is that the wine should be clear rather than cloudy. The depth of colour also tells you about the intensity of the wine. As a general rule the deeper the colour is the more full-bodied the wine will be, although older reds do fade slightly, particularly towards the edges.

Step three

Now swirl the wine in the glass and take a sniff. The movement helps to release the wine's aromas. You should be able to pick up the most dominant aromas in the wine, such as fruit or oak. By and large, the more expensive the wine the more complex its aromas will be, but don't worry to begin with if you can't detect more than one or two. If the wine doesn't smell of much, it might be too cold. If the smell is unpleasant, the wine might be corked (*see* pages 50–1).

Step four

Next take a sip – not too much or you'll be tempted to swallow it immediately. Hold the wine in your mouth and experiment with sucking air in gently as you do so. If you that

difficult, simply move the wine around from front to back and side to side, so all your taste buds get the benefit. You can pick up not only the flavors you detected when you smelled the wine, but its texture too. You'll notice particularly if the wine is sharp, smooth, sweet or oaky.

Step five

Finally swallow the wine (this is the best part). If it's a good wine you'll be able to taste not only the flavors and textures you've already picked up, but other flavors as well. Serious wines have what's called a long finish, or aftertaste, which means you continue tasting them for several seconds after you've swallowed them. If you do want to spit, simply find a bucket or a large bowl, aim and fire. You might dribble to begin with (we all do), but

you get better with practice – in fact, you could try blowing the wine out.

But remember, you'll find the whole exercise easier and a lot more pleasurable if you serve each wine in a decent glass and at the right temperature (*see* pages 46–7).

Organizing a tasting

Tasting with friends or family is a lot more fun than tasting on your own. You simply need to find four to six wines to compare (not more than that or you'll lose track of what the first one tasted like). You can either follow one of the tasting spreads in this book (*see* pages 60–5 and 70–5), or pick a country you're unfamiliar with and try, say, three whites and three reds. Do remember to make a note of those you particularly like.

Why wine tastes the way it does

The more technical side of winemaking might seem a bit of a yawn, but understanding a little about what goes into wine and where and how it's made can not only help you make sense of the descriptions you find on wine labels, but also lead you to the wines you're most likely to enjoy.

The first and easiest bit of information to identify is the grape variety – indeed these days most wines are named after the variety or varieties they're made from. Although the flavor might vary slightly depending on where the grapes are grown (*see* below), the variety gives a wine its defining character. A Chardonnay will no more taste of gooseberries than a Sauvignon will of peaches or ripe mangoes. A Syrah or Shiraz will always be spicier than a Pinot Noir. (Check the main characteristics of each key grape variety on pages 56 to 75.)

The second important factor is climate – how hot or cool is the region where the grapes come from? Hot areas invariably produce riper grapes and richer-tasting wines than cool areas, so on the whole, wines from the (hotter) southern hemisphere are fuller and fruitier than those from cooler parts of France or Germany.

What goes on in the vineyard will affect the taste too: how old the vines are and how large a crop the winemaker gets from them. How the winemaker trains the vines and how radically the foliage is cut back, whether they are sprayed intensively or tries to grow them organically, whether they are harvested early or late. (Get a crash course in grape growing on pages 76–9.)

It also makes a difference who makes the wine – a big company with all the latest high-tech equipment or a small family winemaker with a few barrels in the back of a wooden shack. You only have to think about the differences in food produced by modern factories and small artisanal producers to realize similar variations must exist between wines that are made in different ways. (You can find out more about the options open to winemakers on pages 80–1.)

Another important clue to style is whether a wine is oaked or not, whether a winemaker uses new oak barrels, casks that are decades old, or simply stores the wine in stainless steel tanks. The effects of different oak treatments are discussed on pages 82–3 and you can see for yourself how distinctive the flavors are by following the tasting on pages 84–5.

A final key element which influences the way a wine tastes is how it is aged or matured – whether that's done by the winemaker, by the shop you buy it from, or by youself. (You can find out more about the effects of ageing and the importance of vintages on pages 86–7.)

A lot of these factors are of course reflected in the price of the wine. By and large, inexpensive wines will be produced from high-yielding vines, simply and cleanly fermented and sent straight out. More costly wines reflect the added time, trouble and expense the winemaker has had to invest in producing them.

But nothing beats actually tasting the differences for yourself, which is why a key element of this section is the comparison of different grape varieties through practical tastings. Do remember that this is the fun part. You don't simply have to sit there and read. Crack open those bottles and try the wines for yourself!

White grapes

Above: Chardonnay – the world's most popular white grape variety.

Chardonnay

At times it seems that almost every white wine you come across is made from Chardonnay. Its extraordinary popularity is due to the fact that it can be made in so many parts of the world, in so many styles. Even though people sometimes claim to be bored with Chardonnay, they rarely mean it. One style may pall, but you can always move on to another.

The two biggest influences on Chardonnay are climate and oak. By and large Chardonnays that are made in hotter countries such as Australia and South Africa will taste richer and fruitier than those made in cooler regions such as Burgundy and the north of Italy, simply because the grapes get riper. The kind of citrus and melon flavors you find in Chardonnay from most parts of Europe transform themselves into ripe peach or tropical fruit in hotter regions.

Even in a relatively cool climate, however, Chardonnay's character can be transformed by oak. So much so, in fact, that the buttery, vanilla character people associate with the grape is often the flavor of new oak barrels. The longer you leave Chardonnay in oak for, the bigger, more full-bodied it becomes (*see* pages 82–5). Combine that process with very ripe grapes, as they do in California and Australia, and the result is a whoppingly alcoholic wine of enormous weight and power.

There's also a correlation between the style of Chardonnay and its price. Basically, in places where it grows easily and the winemaker (or more likely big-scale wine producer) can get

Above: The Sauvignon grape grows best in cooler regions.

huge crops from the grapes, the result will be simple and fruity. In cooler areas, on smaller estates, where more time and trouble is taken, you'll get more complex, creamy, nutty wines that will age for several years.

You often find Chardonnay blended with other grape varieties (generally to keep the cost down, but retain the appeal of having Chardonnay on the lable). By and large, you end up with a wine that tastes of Chardonnay, except when it's blended with grapes that have a strong personality of their own, such as Sauvignon or Sémillon. (Sauvignon tends to produce a crisper, more citrussy wine, Sémillon a sweeter, more fruity one.)

Sauvignon Blanc

The most distinctive characteristics of Sauvignon are its tangy acidity and intense, citrussy fruit, which are shown off to best advantage when the wine is drunk fresh and young.

Sauvignon thrives best in cooler areas such as the Loire and the Marlborough region of New Zealand, where you find the most piercingly intense

gooseberry and citrus fruit flavors. Cheaper Sauvignons from other parts of France, Hungary and South Africa tend to be simply lemony, while warmer areas such as Australia and other parts of New Zealand, will bring out a more pronounced citrus peel and tropical fruit character. Put it in oak barrels (a more popular style in California where it is called Fumé Blanc) and it becomes much softer, rounder and more appley – a completely contrasting style.

Riesling

People used to start their wine-drinking experience with Riesling (or wines that masqueraded as Riesling) and ended up growing out of it. Now they discover it and never look back. Once you get over the image problem the flavors of Riesling are hugely

Above: Riesling – a great and seriously underrated grape variety.

Above: Sémillon is used to make sweet as well as dry wines.

appealing, from crisp green apple (the Mosel) to rich lime and tropical fruit (Australia) to the intensely sweet but exquisitely well-balanced dessert wines of Germany, Austria, Canada and New Zealand. Riesling also ages wonderfully well, acquiring intriguing petrolly, kerosene flavors.

Sémillon

Sémillon is one of the unsung heroes of the wine world. Although it makes many of the world's greatest sweet wines (including Sauternes), it's also central to some of the most delicious and distinctive dry whites. It has an appealing fresh pineappley, flavor that can be transformed into roast pineapple and nuts by long ageing. On its own it's at its opulent best in Australia (where they drop the accent on the "e"), and there are some impressive Sémillons coming out of

South Africa. But it is its magically harmonious relationship with Sauvignon that transforms it into the supremely graceful, elegant dry whites

you find in Bordeaux. A grape I predict we'll see a lot more of as drinkers cast around for alternatives to Chardonnay.

Chenin Blanc

Another grape with a split personality, Chenin is mainly used for making fairly basic, medium-bodied dry whites. But with decent grapes and a bit of wizardry in the winery (mainly in South Africa and New Zealand) Chenin can be made to taste as good as Chardonnay. However, it's also capable of producing extraordinarily opulent, honeyed and long-lived sweet wines, as it does in the Loire region of France, and some pretty good sparkling wines.

Colombard

Not one of the world's most exciting grape varieties (except when it's turned into Cognac), but widely planted to produce inexpensive, crisp,

Above: Chenin Blanc is grown mainly in the Loire Valley and South Africa.

Above: Colombard – vigorous and useful.

citrussy whites such as Vin de Pays des Côtes de Gascogne or, in hot climates such as California and Australia, much riper, sweeter, more tropical wines. It is a common blending partner for Chardonnay.

Gewürztraminer

Once you've tasted the exotic rose-petal and lychee flavors of Gewürztraminer you can pick it out blindfolded. It is one of the most distinctive aromatic grapes, it is at its classic best in Alsace, where it makes wines that range from dry to intensely sweet. It is also successfully produced in Hungary, New Zealand, Oregon and South Africa.

Muscat

Surprisingly, this is one of the few grapes that actually tastes of grapes rather than of some other kind of fruit. There are so-called "dry" Muscats (which are actually more off-dry than dry), but the grape is mainly used to make sweet dessert wines such as Muscat de Beaumes-de-Venise or light sparkling wines such as Asti.

Pinot Gris/Pinot Grigio

One grape, two different names, two different styles. Pinot Grigio, which you'll mainly find in Italy, is a crisp, fresh, dry white; Pinot Gris, a speciality of Alsace, is much richer and spicier. New World winemakers in countries such as New Zealand and the United States (Oregon) are going more for the Alsace style, but producing lighter, smoother, peachier wines. Expect to see more of this variety.

Pinot Blanc

A grape that generally produces fairly neutral dry whites, but in the hands of top winemakers in Alsace, Italy (where it's called Pinot Bianco), Austria and Germany (who call it Weissburgunder) it can result in much classier wines.

Verdelho

Originally Portuguese (widely grown in Madeira), but successfully transplanted to Australia, Verdelho is an increasingly popular variety for producing clean, green, limey whites that can last for years. It may also be blended with Chardonnay and Sauvignon.

Viognier

A cult variety that punches well above its weight, Viognier might be temperamental and difficult to grow, but it has such a rare, seductive, ripe-apricot flavor that winemakers can't resist having a crack at it. It is at its best in the tiny Rhône appellation of Condrieu, but good examples are emerging from the Languedoc, California and Australia.

Above: Viognier – gloriously, lushly aromatic, yet flighty and difficult to cultivate.

Tasting Chardonnay

Chardonnay's real character is often obscured by oak (*see* pages 84–5). But to see how different the actual flavor of the grape is try these four unoaked or lightly oaked examples, which show the powerful effect of local conditions. Even though two of the bottles are from the same country, France, they are markedly different, as are the wines from Australia and Chile (despite both countries having very hot climates). Pick bottles from the most recent vintage, remembering that southern hemisphere countries such as Australia and Chile, are six months ahead of France.

Chablis (unoaked)

The classic dry white wine from the north of the Burgundy region in France.

Color: Very light with a slight greenish tinge.

Aroma: What's noticeable is how it doesn't smell nearly as fruity as most modern Chardonnays. The aroma is more minerally (flint is the classic description, but I like to think of it more as wet stones). Some tasters even detect wet wool.

Taste: You'll probably pick up some fruit now, but it's very delicate. Crisp apple and maybe a touch of lemon. There's also a slight creaminess about the wine and possibly a hint of almonds. Then it's quite tart again when you swallow.

Conclusion: A dry, crisp, elegant white wine that is quite unlike other Chardonnays on the market. It may not strike you as the most appealing bottle in the line-up, but it really comes into its own with food.

Similar wines: Petit Chablis (a lesser appellation) has the same minerally character; or try a young basic white burgundy (Bourgogne Blanc).

Vin de Pays d'Oc Chardonnay

A popular varietal (a wine made from a single grape variety) from the warm, sunny Languedoc region in the south of France.

Color: Light straw.

Aroma: Although this is also a French Chardonnay, you can immediately pick up that the fruit is riper than it is in Burgundy. Melons and peaches, rather than apples.

Taste: A much smoother wine than the Chablis, with ripe melon and peach flavors. In fact, it's similar to the sensation of eating a fresh peach – ripe, sweet fruit when you first bite in, then a pleasant sharpness when you swallow.

Conclusion: An easy kind of wine to drink on any occasion. Fine on its own; flexible with food.

Similar wines: Wines from the Languedoc are frequently more similar to those of the New World than the rest of France. Try unoaked or lightly oaked Chardonnays from countries such as Australia or South Africa or, cheaper still, Bulgaria or Hungary.

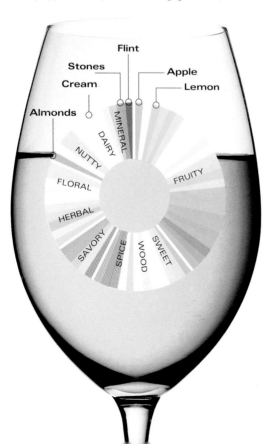

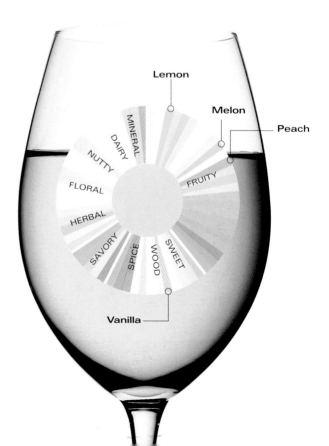

Chardonnay flavor guide

CREAM
More expensive Chardonnays develop a rich, creamy flavor when the wine is left on its lees (*see* pages 80–1).

PEACH
The most obviously recognizable fruit flavor in Chardonnays from warm climates such as southern France.

CITRUS
Chardonnays from cooler growing areas such as the Casablanca Valley in Chile have very pronounced citrus flavors.

Casablanca Chardonnay

A highly regarded cool growing region on the coast of Chile.
Color: Similar to the Vin de Pays d'Oc Chardonnay; light straw.
Aroma: The Casablanca Valley produces wines with a marked lemon and grapefruit character. More fragrant, aromatic and citrussy than the previous Chardonnay – although it might be higher in alcohol.
Taste: Again, the citrus character is really obvious. And you may get a touch of stewed apples and cream. Close your eyes and you could almost be drinking an oaked Sauvignon.
Conclusion: A very refreshing style of Chardonnay – a good alternative if you don't like the super-ripe tropical flavors of the Australian variety. But drink it young.
Similar wines: Other "cool climate" Chardonnays such as those from the Marlborough region of New Zealand.

Southeast Australian Chardonnay

The style most people associate with this grape.
Color: Much richer and more yellowy than the previous wines.
Aroma: Like putting your nose in a bowlful of tropical fruits – mango, paw paw, passion fruit and pineapple.
Taste: Much riper than the other Chardonnays. It feels sweeter and more syrupy (almost like canned peaches) in your mouth. And when you swallow, you're still left with the taste of sweet, sweet fruit.
Conclusion: Australian Chardonnay's great virtue is consistency. This style of wine is blended from grapes taken from several regions to ensure the taste and style remains consistent from year to year.
Similar wines: No place quite matches Australia for such intense tropical fruit flavors. California comes the closest, although its Chardonnays tend to be more heavily oaked.

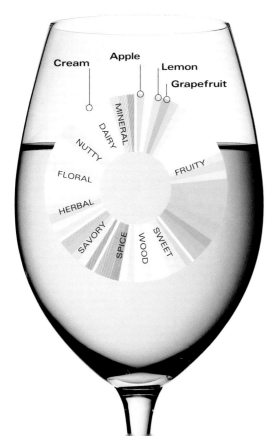

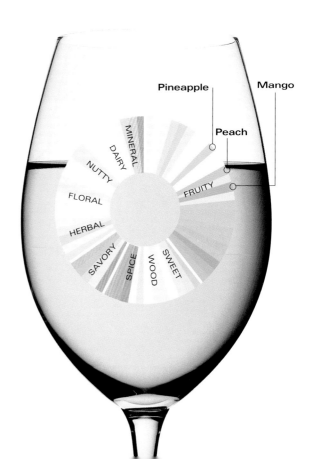

Tasting Sauvignon Blanc

Tasting these four examples of Sauvignon Blanc shows just how diverse this grape variety can be. What puts some people off classic Sauvignons such as Sancerre is their crisp acidity, but that can be modified either by oak (as in the case of Fumé Blanc) or by blending the grape with another variety such as Sémillon (as the French traditionally do in Bordeaux). Additionally, the riper, more tropical fruit you get in the warmer growing conditions in New Zealand produces yet another spectrum of flavors, which you'll find highlighted on the respective flavor wheels.

Sancerre

(Loire Valley, France.) The classic role model for other Sauvignons.
Color: Quite light. What you'd expect from a dry white wine.
Aroma: Very distinctive. The trademark gooseberry fruit of Sauvignon Blanc should be well in evidence, but there's also a slightly aromatic note of blackcurrant leaves and hints of flintiness. You can tell this wine is going to be crisp.
Taste: What immediately hits you is the acidity. It shouldn't be sour, just very sharp and clean, like a lemon sherbet.

The gooseberry fruit is there though, to stop it tasting too lean. And the effect is much less marked once you try it with food.
Conclusion: You might notice differences between one bottle and another, depending on the vintage and the quality of the producer. At its best this is the most stylish type of Sauvignon around (though not always the best value for the money).
Similar wines: Other Loire Sauvignons, such as Pouilly-Fumé, Menetou-Salon and Quincy.

New Zealand Sauvignon Blanc

(Marlborough.) Generally considered to be the best example of Sauvignon in the New World.
Color: Straw with hints of green.
Aroma: Here the fruit is more intense and noticeably riper than that of the Sancerre – dessert rather than cooking gooseberries. You may also pick up notes of pineapple, lime and tropical fruits, as well as slightly sappy aromas such as grass, green peppers, asparagus and even nettles.

Taste: Again, much more intense and less acidic than a Loire Sauvignon. A pure blast of gooseberry, tropical and citrus fruit which lingers long after you've swallowed.
Conclusion: Much rounder in style and more powerfully flavored than the Sancerre – on the other hand, it doesn't have Sancerre's fine balance and delicacy.
Similar wines: No place quite matches this style for pungency, but try South Africa and the few Sauvignons produced in Australia.

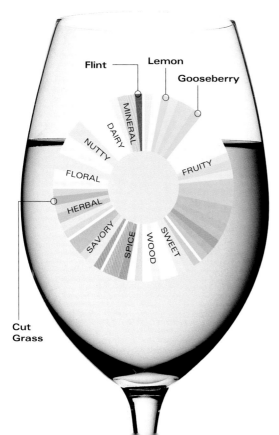

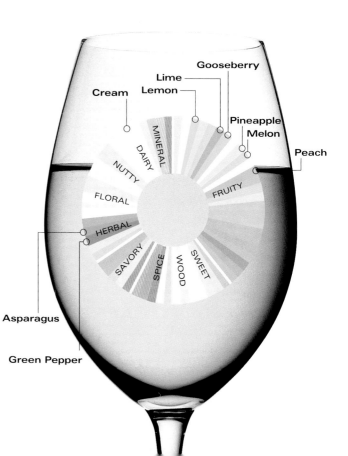

Sauvignon Blanc flavor guide

GRASS
There's a green, herbaceous grassy note in many Sauvignons, particularly those from the Loire Valley in France.

GOOSEBERRY
The distinctive aroma of gooseberries is the most easily recognizable characteristic of the Sauvignon grape.

LEMON
Some Sauvignons, such as those from Bordeaux, taste quite lemony. In warmer areas this can seem more like lemon peel.

White Bordeaux

Sauvignon blended with Sémillon and possibly a small percentage of Muscadelle.

Color: Light straw, verging on gold.

Aroma: A cocktail of fruit aromas, particularly peach and pineapple – the characteristic smell of Sémillon (how dominant this is depends on the blend). Not much gooseberry, but you may just be able to pick up those nettley, grassy, Sauvignon aromas.

Taste: White Bordeaux manages to be light and lush at the same time. A touch of oak gives it a smooth creaminess but the overall impression is of ripe, juicy, peachy fruit.

Conclusion: This is one of those marriages made in heaven. The Sémillon knocks the sharper edges off the Sauvignon; the Sauvignon adds a refreshing crispness to the Sémillon. One of the most underrated and elegant white wines around, that has the ability to age for several years.

Similar wines: All Sauvignon/Sémillon blends will have something of this quality.

California Fumé Blanc

Oak adding softness to a lighter style of Sauvignon.

Color: Light straw.

Aroma: Much softer and less assertive in style than the other three Sauvignons. Soft, stewed apple and lemon aromas, with touches of marzipan and spice. You probably wouldn't recognize this as a Sauvignon if you tasted it blind (without seeing the label).

Taste: Again, there should be that distinctive, sweetish, stewed apple fruit, possibly with a touch of candied lemon or grapefruit peel. But the presence of oak is softening the overall effect of the wine and adding a slightly spicy flavor at the end as you swallow.

Conclusion: A totally contrasting style to the other Sauvignons that might be more accessible to first-time drinkers. Very popular in the United States, but less so in Europe.

Similar wines: Other softer, dry whites, like more traditional styles of Rueda from Spain.

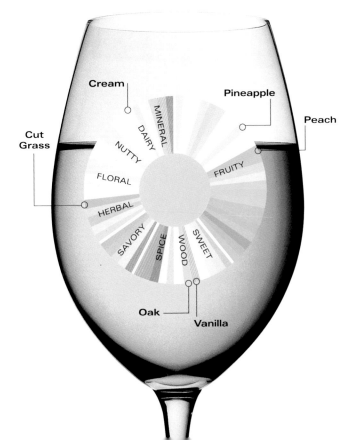

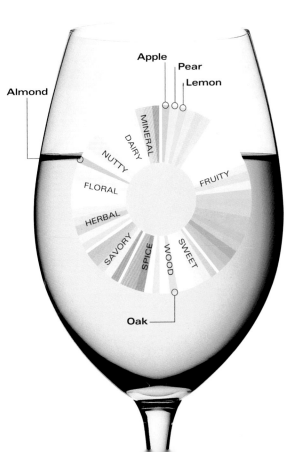

Tasting Riesling

Tasting a Riesling isn't easy. Many Rieslings take a year or two to settle down after bottling before they start to reveal their true character. To make it easier for yourself – and to get an idea of the intriguing petrolly flavors the grape develops – pick bottles from the previous rather than the current vintage, i.e. wines that are one to two years old (even three or more in the case of Alsace Riesling). The flavors you encounter may be unfamiliar, but Riesling is well worth persevering with for its particularly pure fruit flavors – quite unlike anything else the wine world has to offer.

Mosel Kabinett Riesling

A classic German Riesling.

Color: Very light, almost like water.

Aroma: The distinctive floral (white flower) aromas sometimes make you overlook just how fruity this style of Riesling is. But, depending on how ripe the grapes are, you might be able to pick out any one of the following: green apple, lemon, grape or white peach. And there's often a minerally note to the wine too.

Taste: Deliciously light and juicy – like biting into a perfectly ripe grape.

Conclusion: One of the most refreshing styles of white wine you can find – and at around eight percent ABV, blissfully low in alcohol. Develops a marked petrolly character with age.

Similar wines: Try a dry Spätlese Riesling, still delicate, but with slightly riper fruit flavors (*see* pages 104–7).

Alsace Riesling

More scarce and frequently more expensive than German Riesling, but well worth seeking out.

Color: Light straw.

Aroma: There's a characteristic spiciness about Alsace wines that you should be able to pick up when you swirl the wine around. And the fruit is noticeably riper than the Mosel: Cox or Blenheim apples rather than Granny Smiths.

Taste: Recognizably Riesling with a delicious streak of citrussy acidity, but with some softer, richer fruit flavors too. And always that slight hint of muskiness.

Conclusion: The extra four degrees of alcohol (most Alsace Rieslings are around 12 percent) make a big difference. A much weightier, spicier Riesling than the German variety, which – particularly in the case of the best wines – needs several years to develop.

Similar wines: Austrian Rieslings are quite similar to those from Alsace.

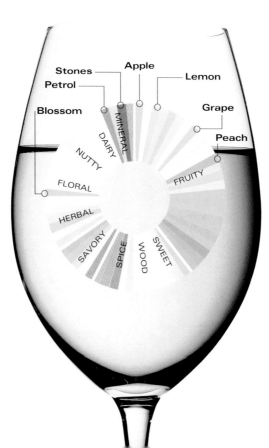

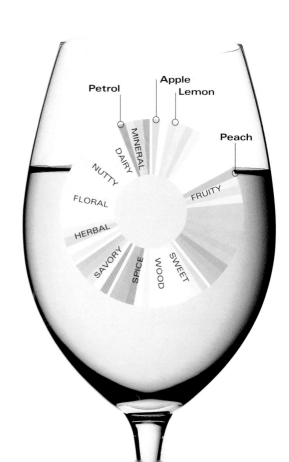

Riesling flavor guide

APPLE
Young Rieslings, particularly those from the Mosel, often taste and smell of crunchy green apples.

LIME
Rieslings from warmer countries, such as Australia, are higher in alcohol and have noticably richer limey flavors.

PETROL
As Rieslings age, they often develop an aroma of petrol or kerosene – fortunately much more attractive than it sounds.

New Zealand Marlborough Riesling

One of the cooler wine-growing areas of New Zealand, well-suited to Riesling grapes.

Color: Pale gold.

Aroma: Slightly more floral and fragrant than Australian Riesling. Distinctively citrussy with maybe a hint of lychees or tropical fruit.

Taste: Depending on the producer and the vintage, the flavors can range from citrus (lemon and grapefruit) and apple to ripe peach and passion fruit. But the overall effect is much softer, less mouth-tinglingly racy than a German or Alsace Riesling.

Conclusion: An underrated source of Riesling that could become as successful for Marlborough as Sauvignon Blanc.

Similar wines: North American Rieslings from New York, Oregon and Canada are the closest in style.

Australian Clare Valley Riesling

Along with the Eden Valley, the prime growing area for Australian Rieslings.

Color: Greenish gold.

Aroma: Unmistakably, gloriously, limey.

Taste: Much zestier than any other style of Riesling. Really powerful lime and lemon peel flavors. Apple and lemon, too, but they come through as an aftertaste. And you'll get that unmistakable kerosene note as the wine ages.

Conclusion: A classic Australian wine – vigorous, zesty, uncomplicated and enjoyable. And remarkably good with fashionable Pacific Rim and southeast Asian food.

Similar wines: No other Riesling has quite that limey intensity.

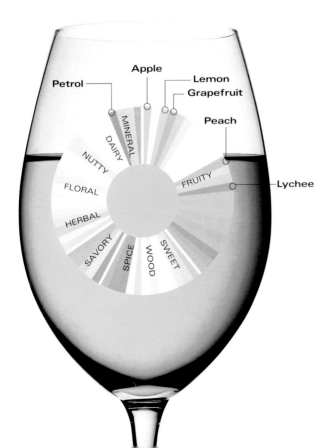

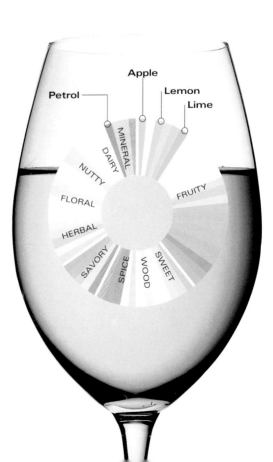

Red grapes

Cabernet Sauvignon

Cabernet Sauvignon is the Chardonnay of the red-wine world – a grape that's planted virtually everywhere and that produces wine at every price, from the inexpensive oak-aged Cabernets of Bulgaria to the great First Growths of Bordeaux.

Although Cabernet's character is affected by oak ageing, it's more influenced by climate. In cooler areas such as Bordeaux, South Africa and New Zealand, it's relatively light and fruity – you can sometimes pick up quite a leafy, green-peppery flavor, rather than the super-ripe, concentrated blackcurrant fruit you find in warmer areas such as Chile, California and Australia. To counteract this, Cabernet is often blended with another grape variety to soften it and round it out. Generally that's Merlot, but in Australia Cabernet is frequently and successfully blended with Shiraz.

Because Cabernet is quite tannic it ages well. The effect of barrel-ageing is to make it mellow, smoother and more plummy and to give it – particularly in Bordeaux – a distinctive cedary, cigar-box character.

Merlot

Cabernet might be widely admired, but Merlot is much more lovable. With its soft, rich, velvety fruit, it has to be one of the most enjoyable red wines in the world.

Like Cabernet, Merlot is widely planted. Nowadays it's the basis of most inexpensive Bordeaux as well as the main grape variety used for the

Above: Cabernet Sauvignon makes some of the world's most long-lived red wines.

Above: Merlot produces wines that are particularly soft and supple.

wines of the region's so-called right bank, St-Emilion and Pomerol. It also does well in neighboring Spain and down in the Languedoc, where it's proved popular with visiting Australian winemakers. Lighter, fruitier versions are produced in Italy and Hungary.

In the New World Merlot has found a natural home in Chile and in California, where winemakers have become quite besotted with it. Some top-quality Merlots are also being produced in Washington, and it's being increasingly widely planted in New Zealand and in South Africa. It's hard to see Merlot falling out of fashion, given its ability to deliver the particularly soft, fruity reds that people want to drink these days.

Pinot Noir

One of the world's most tricky and temperamental grapes, Pinot Noir is a nightmare for winemakers. When it's good, as it can be in Burgundy and on the West Coast, it makes the most ethereal, delicately fruity red wines in the world. When it's poor (usually also in Burgundy), it can be thin, sharp and weedy.

Even within Burgundy it can be made in an extraordinary variety of styles, depending on the quality of the vineyard, the weather and the winemaker. While basic red burgundy is generally light and raspberryish, a top Burgundian Pinot Noir such as Vosne-Romanée can be quite full-bodied. What is unique about Pinot Noir in Burgundy is a fine silken texture that no other country quite emulates. The Californians get nearest to it and there are some fine examples – at a price – from Oregon, Canada, Australia, New Zealand, Germany, Austria and Switzerland.

Less expensively, some cheerfully fruity Pinots are emerging from Chile, Spain and the Languedoc, while Romania produces its own particularly rustic version. Just to underline Pinot's versatility, it's also one of the major components of Champagne and other top sparkling wines.

Above: Pinot Noir – one of the trickiest grapes for winemakers to handle.

Above: Syrah is known as Shiraz in Australia.

Syrah/Shiraz

The two names for the Syrah/Shiraz grape reflect a big dividing line in style. As the mainstay of the wines of the Rhône, Syrah produces wines that are rich, dense, spicy and sometimes gamy in character. Shiraz, its New World incarnation, is altogether sweeter, fruitier and more exuberant.

Throughout most of the south of France – the southern Rhône and the Languedoc – Syrah is traditionally not used on its own but blended, most commonly with Grenache (*see* right), Mourvèdre (an interesting grape in its own right), Cinsault and Carignan to create full-bodied yet supple reds. In the northern Rhône Syrah is used on its own to make big, spicy, peppery wines such as Cornas, Hermitage, St-Joseph and the seductively elegant Côte-Rôtie.

Hermitage has been the model for the Australians, who have annexed Shiraz and made it virtually their national wine. No one else produces Shiraz of quite such power and sweetness – watch out, though, for Argentina, which has the right climate to pull it off.

Grenache

You may be surprised to know that Grenache, not Cabernet, is the world's most widely planted red-wine grape. It has a deceptively sweet strawberry taste that disguises its frequently high levels of alcohol.

Grenache underpins most southern French reds and is generally the dominant grape in Côtes du Rhône and Châteauneuf-du-Pape. It is also widely planted in Spain where it's known as Garnacha. It has recently come to prominence in its own right because the Australians have rediscovered its virtues and are making some magnificently concentrated wines in much the same style as Shiraz. There's also a following in California. Grenache is not a great grape but it is very, very good – and certainly on its way up.

Sangiovese

There's a revival of interest in Italian grape varieties* and Sangiovese is at the heart of it. This is the grape that makes Chianti and most of Tuscany's reds. Like many Italian grapes it has a high level of acidity and needs oak – or another grape variety such as Cabernet, to smooth out the sharp edges. But Sangiovese produces delightfully supple, elegant wines that go exceptionally well with food. Increasingly, the grape is featured on labels in its own right, especially in the New World, where it has fans in California, Argentina and Australia. (*Others include Barbera, Bonarda, Dolcetto and Nebbiolo, the grape that makes Barolo and Barbaresco.*)

Tempranillo

Another grape that deserves wider recognition, this time from Spain. Tempranillo is the most important grape in the top wine-growing areas of Rioja and Ribera del Duero (where it's called Tinto Fino). Traditionally, it spends a long time in oak barrels, which gives it an appealing, soft strawberry jam flavor; but many producers are now producing younger, unoaked versions that are more vibrantly fruity. There's not much interest in Tempranillo outside Spain, although Argentina could prove a promising source.

Above: Cabernet Franc is well suited to cooler climates.

Cabernet Franc

A useful variety that can produce ripe grapes in cooler growing regions. It's widely used as a blending component in Bordeaux (it ripens earlier than Cabernet Sauvignon) and on its own in the Loire in stylish light reds such as Chinon and Bourgueil. It also does well in northern Italy. In character Cabernet Franc is not dissimilar to its more famous namesake, but it's more fragrant and herbal – you can pick it out even if only a small amount has been used in a blend. It can also be used to make quite substantial full-bodied wines, a style more favored by New World countries such as Austrália, New Zealand and South Africa.

Gamay

One of the brightest, breeziest, fruitiest grapes around, Gamay is used to produce Beaujolais. In general, Gamay is made without oak, so that nothing gets in the way of all that juicy raspberry and bubblegum flavor, though it is capable of making quite serious wines similar in style to a top burgundy. It is also found in the Loire region of France and Switzerland.

Pinotage

A home-grown South African variety that produces a range of styles from light gluggable, occasionally rubbery, reds to rich tarry, spicy monsters. One of the best-value, full-bodied reds around. Some is grown in New Zealand, though not much is exported.

Zinfandel

The much-loved grape of California, that again covers a wide spectrum of wines, from medium-dry "white Zin" to "killer Zins" of enormous extraction and power, but which nevertheless retain a particularly appealing sweet, brambly fruit. A few winemakers are experimenting with it in Australia and South Africa.

Above: Exuberantly fruity Gamay is the grape that is used to make Beaujolais.

Tasting Cabernet Sauvignon

Cabernet is a grape that really divides Old World and New World wine-drinkers. Traditionalists find New World wines too sweet and jammy, modernists often find Bordeaux too tough and tannic. Here are four examples so you can see which style appeals to you. The two cheaper wines, the Bordeaux and the Chilean examples, show the contrasts in Cabernets from totally different climates. With the more expensive Australian and Californian wines, the picture is complicated by oak, but in the Coonawarra example you can see the strong effect of *terroir* (climate and soil).

Bordeaux (Médoc)

Likely to be a blend of Cabernet Sauvignon and Merlot – possibly with some Cabernet Franc, but this depends on the vintage.

Color: Quite light. The color of red plums.

Aroma: The fruit character is quite subtle, mingling with woody aromas – cedar, cigar boxes, tobacco or pencil shavings (depending on which you're most familiar with). Some more modern styles of Bordeaux may have a more obvious toasty oak character.

Taste: You can pick out the blackcurrant fruit, but the overall effect is quite light and elegant. You might have a slightly furred-up feeling in your mouth after you swallow – that's the tannin – but it's not so noticeable when you drink the wine with food.

Conclusion: Bordeaux varies markedly from vintage to vintage. In some years it will taste quite ripe and fruity; in others you may pick up slightly herbaceous green pepper or green bean flavors.

Similar wines: Bordeaux is quite a cool area for Cabernet. You tend to find similar wines in other relatively cool regions, such as northern Italy and Hawke's Bay in New Zealand.

Chilean Cabernet Sauvignon

Chile is one of the best inexpensive sources of Cabernet in the New World.

Color: Much lighter and brighter than Bordeaux.

Aroma: Very pure blackcurrant and blackberry aromas and not much noticeable oak – in the cheaper Cabernets at least. (Reserve wines will taste fuller and oakier.)

Taste: The most noticeable difference from the Médoc is the feel in your mouth, this wine is much, much richer and softer, without any harsh tannins.

Conclusion: Although the alcohol content is broadly similar to that of Bordeaux, the flavor couldn't be more different, which illustrates how much riper Cabernet gets in a really warm climate. Best drunk young to get the full impact of that lovely, vivid fruit.

Similar wines: No place quite matches Chile at the price for ripe fruit, but try South Africa.

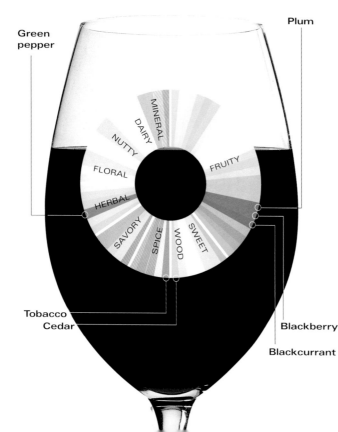

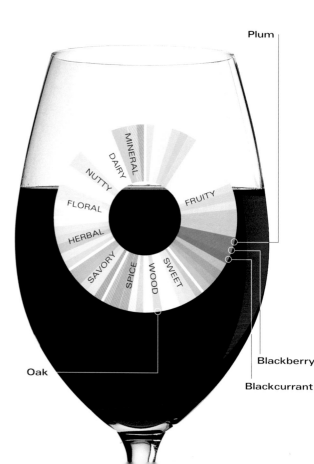

Cabernet Sauvignon flavor guide

BLACKCURRANT
This is the most characteristic fruit flavor of the Cabernet Sauvignon grape, especially in younger wines.

MINT
Mint or eucalyptus flavors are particularly noticeable in Cabernets from South Australia, especially the Coonawarra region.

TOBACCO
Oak-aged Cabernets often develop cedary, tobacco-like aromas, sometimes also identified as pencil shavings or cigar box.

Californian Cabernet Sauvignon

Originally modeled on Bordeaux, Californian Cabernet now has a strong identity of its own. The most striking examples come from the Napa and Sonoma Valleys.

Color: Dark plum.

Aroma: A powerful, heady aroma of ripe blackcurrant fruit, mingling with vanilla oak.

Taste: A big, macho, muscular style of Cabernet – very smooth, very rich, very solid. More obviously oaky than any of the other Cabernets, but with sumptuously sweet fruit to balance it.

Conclusion: Unmistakably a full-bodied, rather than a medium-bodied wine, with which you really need food to enjoy it at its best. Don't drink it too young – the oak needs time to integrate.

Similar wines: There are quite a few top, expensive, oak-aged Cabernets now emerging from Spain and Italy that show a similarly impressive concentration.

Coonawarra Cabernet Sauvignon

A distinctive style of Cabernet from the Coonawarra region of South Australia.

Color: Deep, rich red.

Aroma: The first thing you'll notice is a strong smell of eucalyptus almost masking the intensely sweet blackcurrant fruit.

Taste: Extraordinarily opulent, velvety, ultra-ripe fruit – almost like cassis (blackcurrant) syrup. But the mint character and the oak (which you hardly notice) prevent it tasting too sweet.

Conclusion: As powerful as a Californian Cabernet, but even fruitier. You can really pick up a specific Coonawarra character in those eucalyptus flavors.

Similar wines: Coonawarra Cabernet is expensive, but you can find the same sweet, jammy fruit in other southeast and southern Australian Cabernets and Cabernet/Shiraz blends. If you enjoy this style, McLaren Vale is another region to look for.

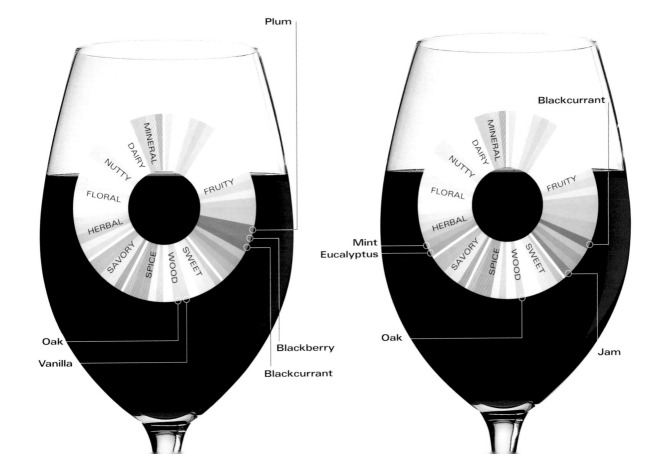

Tasting Pinot Noir

This is the trickiest of all the tastings and, I'm afraid, the most expensive. But it's worth the investment to discover what the fuss is about burgundy, the ultimate expression of Pinot Noir. Pinot varies so maddeningly from producer to producer, and from one year to the next, that it's hard to predict what you'll find when you open the bottle. The best advice I can give is to find a good wine merchant, explain what you're trying to do, and let them suggest four wines to try. The bad news is that once you develop a taste for Pinot Noir, you're hooked for life.

Bourgogne Pinot Noir

The most basic kind of red burgundy – which may, however, be a cut above average if it comes from a good producer. Pick a recent vintage.

Color: Light, cherry red, fading to pink at the rim.

Aroma: Pure, sweet raspberry fruit. There's not a lot else going on.

Taste: Deliciously light and fruity – but quite tart, like berries pulled straight off the bush (sometimes it can be too sharp).

Conclusion: This is Pinot at its simplest and purest. Unoaked. Designed to be drunk young rather than kept. At its best it's delightful.

Similar wines: Other inexpensive Pinots in this style come from the Languedoc, but Beaujolais (which is made from Gamay) is probably a closer alternative due to its simple fruit character. Also try similarly light juicy Italian reds such as Bardolino and Valpolicella.

Gevrey-Chambertin

One of the great (or at least it should be great) burgundies from the Côte de Nuits. Buy one which is at least three, and preferably five, years old.

Color: A deeper red than the basic burgundy, but it still has a translucent quality.

Aroma: You can immediately sense that this is a much richer, more powerful wine. The fruit is concentrated, sweet and ripe – cherries, mulberries and plums rather than raspberries.

Taste: Soft, supple fruit, supported by high-quality oak – not obvious but you get that recognizable spicy aftertaste.

Older vintages will show greater complexity – you may find hints of mushrooms, truffles, game – even slightly farm-yardy aromas.

Conclusion: The most beguiling quality about good burgundy is its delicate sweetness and fine silky texture, but a wine of this high quality needs time to get there.

Similar wines: Although varied in style, other top burgundies will give you this intense satisfaction. Nuits-St-Georges is similarly full-bodied; Vosne-Romanée and Chambolle-Musigny more exotically perfumed.

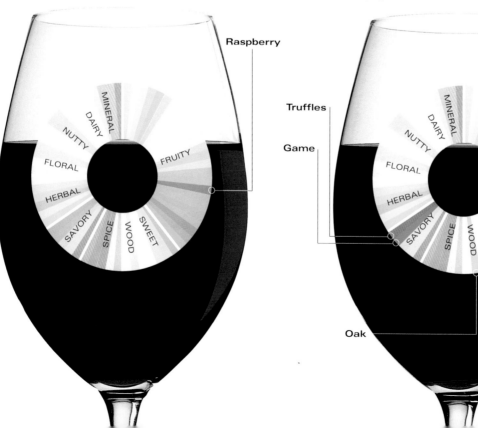

Pinot Noir flavor guide

STRAWBERRY
In warmer climates such as Chile or California, you may detect a hint of strawberries or strawberry jam.

RASPBERRY
Young Pinot Noirs, particularly those from Burgundy, have a particularly pure raspberry flavor.

TRUFFLE
As Pinot Noir ages, it often develops a delicious aroma of truffles that makes it a natural accompaniment to game.

California Pinot Noir

One of the best sources of Pinot Noir in the New World – generally from the cooler coastal regions such as Carneros.

Color: Light, bright cherry red, like young burgundy.

Aroma: Opulent, sweet, ripe raspberry fruit – even a touch perfumed.

Taste: Much riper and sweeter than the fruit you get in Burgundy. The oak is likely to be more obvious – you may be able to pick up vanilla – the overall effect much softer and more rounded.

Conclusion: It might not have quite the depth or velvety texture of the best burgundies, but California Pinot is a lot more reliable. A very good starting point for any Pinot Noir novice.

Similar wines: Any of the New World's other top spots for Pinot Noir – Oregon, New Zealand, the Yarra Valley in Australia – though you will find some producers deliberately make their wines in a richer, more full-bodied style.

Romanian Pinot Noir

A distinctively oaky style of Pinot Noir – quite different from the other three. Pick a reserve.

Color: Dark brick red, fading towards the edge of the glass.

Aroma: Preserved rather than fresh fruit. Plums, raisins and strawberries rather than raspberries.

Taste: Quite delicate strawberry jam flavors with a hint of fruitcake. The soft, sweet, raisiny taste you get from extended oak ageing.

Conclusion: Remarkably good value for money, but it doesn't have the seductive qualities the Pinot Noir devotee is looking for. (That might change if Romania modernizes its wine industry.)

Similar wines: Other oaky wines rather than other Pinots. Bulgarian Cabernet Sauvignon, Valdepeñas, Rioja, southern Italian reds such as Copertino, or, if you want to spoil yourself, Chateau Musar.

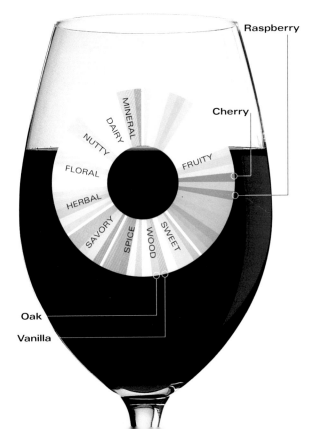

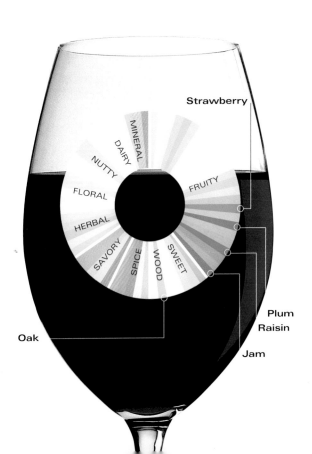

Tasting Syrah/Shiraz

Syrah/Shiraz has such a strong personality that it's less affected than other grapes by variations in climate. Although these examples come from different regions and are made in different ways, you can pick up a clear family resemblance – not least the strong peppery aftertaste. The principal influence upon Syrah/Shiraz is the way it is made. If the vines are allowed to crop too much it can taste quite light and thin, but if yields are kept down (*see* pages 76–7) it can be wonderfully rich and spicy (in this way it resembles other potentially powerful varieties such as Grenache, Pinotage and Zinfandel).

Syrah Vin de Pays d'Oc

New World-style Syrah from the Languedoc region of southern France.

Color: Light, bright, almost jewel-like red.

Aroma: There's always something quite savory about Syrah which you'll pick up in all but the lightest examples. You might be able to detect touches of leather, smoke and tar. But there should be some sweet fruit too – mainly plums.

Taste: Sweet, warm and supple. Despite the fact that it rarely rises above 12.5 percent alcohol, it tastes a lot bigger and spicier than that. Note the peppery aftertaste.

Conclusion: Vin de Pays vary quite significantly between one producer and another, and from vintage to vintage, but you should be able to see the resemblance to the St-Joseph (*see* right).

Similar wines: If you like this style of wine, you're in luck. Syrah is used on its own or blended with other grapes such as Grenache all over the Languedoc and the Rhône to make spicy, full-bodied reds. (*See also* page 68.)

St-Joseph

A typical wine from the northern Rhône, Syrah's heartland.

Color: Full, rich crimson.

Aroma: Exotic complex aromas of violets, plums, leather, oak, and possibly even some earthy, mineral notes. Plus a touch of gameyness in older vintages.

Taste: Very concentrated and spicy. In fact, the spicy character may well dominate the fruit. And note that incredibly strong flavor of black pepper after you swallow.

Conclusion: This is Syrah at its meatiest and most macho. The ideal wine for steak.

Similar wines: Other wines from the northern Rhône – Hermitage, Cornas and, if you want to indulge yourself, Côte-Rôtie. Châteauneuf-du-Pape (though it contains other grapes apart from Syrah) can be similarly full-bodied.

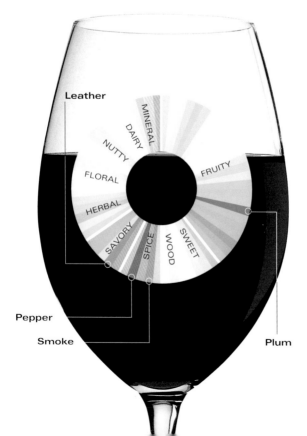

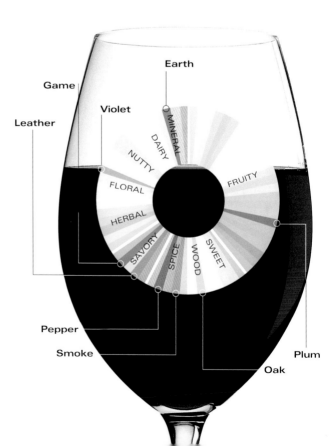

Syrah and Shiraz flavor guide

PLUM
Ripe plum is the most obvious fruit flavor in Syrah or Shiraz, especially the more full-bodied examples.

PEPPER
You can often pick up the flavor of pepper when you taste a Syrah wine, particularly those from the Rhône.

LEATHER
Mature Syrah can often develop quite gamy, leathery notes, sometimes referred to as "sweaty saddle." Modern wines are less likely to have them.

Argentinian Syrah

An exciting, new and inexpensive source of Syrah. But pick a recent vintage.

Color: Rich, plummy.

Aroma: Very ripe, sweet, red berry fruit, though on some wines you get more of a dried fruit character – raisins, currants and prunes. It's less gamey than the other Syrahs.

Taste: Noticeably riper and softer than the French Syrahs, though not quite as sweet or concentrated as an Aussie Shiraz. But again you should be able to pick up the pepper.

Conclusion: Argentinian Syrah, like the wine industry itself, is in a state of evolution. Traditional, heavily oaked styles are being replaced with much more vivid, fruity wines. One to watch for.

Similar wines: As a halfway-house between the Rhône and Australia, it doesn't have an exact equivalent. South African Shiraz comes the nearest.

South Australian Shiraz

The prime growing area for Shiraz in Australia. Try and find one from the Barossa Valley or McLaren Vale.

Color: Rich, deep, highly concentrated red.

Aroma: Very intense, sweet fruit – dark cherries, mulberries and plums – combined with a tarry chocolate character.

Taste: Pure, sweet, lush concentrated fruit buttressed with a big wallop of spicy oak. As peppery as the St-Joseph, but you don't notice it as much because of the fruit.

Conclusion: A good deal of Australian Shiraz reaches 14 percent alcohol, but there's a lovely sweetness and suppleness about them (particularly those from McLaren Vale) that make them seductively easy to drink.

Similar wines: You get the same jammy sweetness in inexpensive Southeast Australian Shiraz, which is often blended with Cabernet or Grenache. Hunter Valley Shiraz has quite a gamy, leathery character, more like that of the northern Rhône.

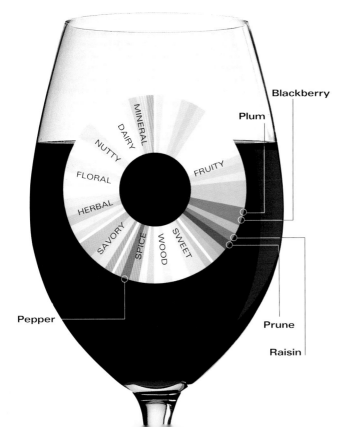

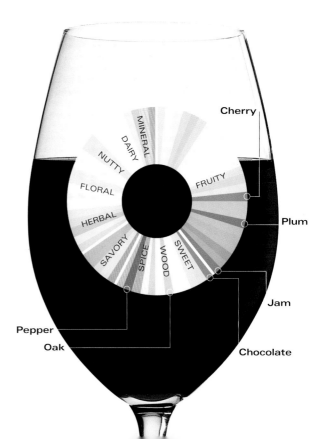

Grape growing

Visit any winery, anywhere in the world, and the owner will tell you that, essentially, good wine is made in the vineyard. And it's true. Without quality grapes, whatever technical wizardry you have at your disposal will get you nowhere. Here are the key factors that enable you to produce them.

Above: The Roxburgh estate, belonging to Rosemount, in the Upper Hunter Valley, has an altitude of 820 feet and is one of Australia's finest vineyards.

Where you plant your vineyard

Obviously that partly depends what you can afford to pay (vineyards cost far more in a famous area than in an undiscovered one); that aside, some sites are much better than others. The main things that count are the amount of rainfall (not too much), the number of sunlight hours (as many as possible), the altitude and the soil. If you want to make an inexpensive wine, you make it easy for the vines and plant on a fertile valley floor. If you want to make a fine wine (i.e. with smaller quantities of concentrated juice), you make the vines struggle by planting them on poor soil or on a slope. Some soils also add their own flavor to the wine – for example, the minerally limestone soils of Chablis.

What grape varieties you plant

You should plant a variety that suits the climate. There's no point in putting a late-ripening variety such as Cabernet Sauvignon in a cool area where it will struggle to ripen. You can also pick a specific strain or "clone" of that grape variety to make your wine in a particular style – for example, to make a Chardonnay taste like white burgundy.

How you tend your vines

Looking after vines is a bit like gardening. If you leave them they just run amok. What you have to do is shape them – usually training them along wires, rather than growing them as bushes. Either way you need to keep the vegetation under control. You want the plant's energy to go into producing grapes rather than leaves – though not too many bunches or you won't get enough concentration.

The other big issue is whether to irrigate or not, a practice frowned on in countries such as France because it can dilute the flavor of the wine. But most French wine-growing regions have more than enough rain. In dry areas, such as Argentina or Australia, vines would simply die without water.

The weather

The weather is one aspect of the equation you can't control. It's not simply a matter of rain during the harvest (which can split ripe grapes and cause them to rot). Heavy frosts can damage buds in the spring; rain at flowering time (yes, vines flower) can inhibit fertilization; high winds can break down plants and hail can wipe out a whole crop. In the end it's a matter of luck. Which is why people prefer to grow grapes in more reliably warm climates rather than cool, marginal ones.

When to harvest

This is always an agonizing decision. You need to leave your grapes long enough to ripen, but the longer you leave them, the more you risk them becoming spoiled. The right moment varies for different wines. For sparkling wines that need a fairly acid base, you don't want your grapes too ripe. For sweet wines you want to leave them on the vine for as long as possible, in some cases until they rot. Most wines fall somewhere in between, with red grapes generally allowed to hang on longer than white. For reds you want ripeness, for whites freshness.

Whether to hand or machine pick

Hand-picking sounds as if it's a better option, but unless you're producing a top-level wine, such as a dessert wine, where you have to select individual berries, that isn't necessarily the case. In fact, this is more likely to be a pragmatic decision, based on whether there is an available labor force to do it (yes, in South America; no, in Australia) and whether the vineyards make it possible. (You couldn't send machines up the precipitous slopes of the Mosel or the Douro, for example.) Most grapes for inexpensive wines are now machine harvested, the big advantage being that you can harvest at night, which keeps the grapes cool and fresh.

Below: Snow covers the village of Le Mesnil-sur-Oger and the small, walled Clos du Mesnil. Owned by Krug, the *clos* (vineyard) is planted entirely with Chardonnay and makes one of the world's most expensive Champagnes.

Organic wines

No longer regarded as the peculiar fringe of winemaking, organic wines, like organic food, are becoming increasingly popular. In order to have his wines certified as organic a producer can't use chemical sprays such as pesticides, fungicides, or fertilizers in the vineyard. Other precautions must be taken such as the use of "cover crops," which encourage insects to kill off the pests and predators.

Not everyone can manage to make wine to these rigorous standards, particularly in regions that have damp or unpredictable climates. If it's a question of losing your entire harvest or being able to put "organic" on your label, most winemakers will naturally choose quite literally to stop the rot.

Nevertheless, a lot more producers now try to keep the use of chemicals to a minimum, both in the vineyard and in the winery. And some of the bigger wine companies, such as Penfolds and Fetzer, have given impetus to the organic movement by bringing out their own range of organic wines.

Below: Planting cover crops, such as wildflowers, is a natural way of ridding the soil of harmful pests as shown here in one of Burgundy's most famous vineyards, La Romanée-Conti.

The most extreme manifestation of organic winemaking is "biodynamics," in which the winemaker determines when the vines are pruned and harvested according to phases of the moon. Instead of using chemicals, adherents treat their soil with homeopathic products such as ground up fish bones and infusions of nettles and chamomile. It might sound like hocus-pocus, but a number of serious winemakers abide by these principles, among them Leroy in Burgundy, Didier Dagueneau in the Loire Valley (Pouilly-Fumé), Chapoutier in the Rhône and James Millton in New Zealand. But their wines inevitably are not cheap.

In the winery, organic winemaking tends to involve lower levels of sulphur (some is essential to protect the wine against air and potentially harmful bacteria) and a minimal use of other additives. In fact, the kind of people who make organic wine generally use other traditional winemaking techniques, such as using wild yeasts and leaving their wines unfiltered (*see* pages 82-3). Wines that

Above: Vineyards of Domaine de Trévallon near Les Baux in Provence. Vineyards with dry, rocky soils, such as these, are not as susceptible to rot and disease as those in damper, cooler regions such as Burgundy and the Loire.

are described as vegetarian or vegan will not have had any animal products used during fining (the process of removing solid particles from the finished wine). This eliminates the use of egg whites, casein (milk protein) and isinglass (fish bladder).

Winemaking

The process of winemaking is basically very simple. You crush the grapes, and the sugar in the juice ferments to alcohol. If you want to make good wine, rather than a vaguely alcoholic liquid, it gets a bit more sophisticated than that. The options depend on the desired style and color.

Red or white?

With white wine, you press the grapes first and then ferment the juice. Grapes for red wine, however, have the skins left in to give the wine color and tannin (the compound that gives red wine its structure).

A single variety or a blend?

Some grapes, such as Riesling and Pinot Noir, which have a fine, delicate flavor, are best used on their own. Others, such as Cabernet, Merlot or Sauvignon and Sémillon, naturally complement each other. A winemaker may use more than one variety to make the wine more complex or simply to keep the cost down; for example, by blending a less expensive variety (such as Colombard) with a pricier one such as Chardonnay.

Wild or cultured yeasts?

Historically, the fermentation process was activated by natural yeasts in the atmosphere, and on the skins of the grapes. Most winemakers now prefer to use cultured yeasts for reliability. Some, however, make a feature of the fact that they use wild yeasts, which give more individual flavors.

Dry or sweet?

If you allow the fermentation to continue until all the sugar in your grapes is converted to alcohol, you get a dry wine. If you stop it at any stage before that, you get a sweeter one. You can also adjust the sweetness of a wine by adding sugar (chaptalisation), a technique used in cooler wine regions where the grapes don't get so ripe. Sweetened grape juice concentrate can also be added (which is what the Germans tend to do). Most dessert wines, by contrast, are made from ultra-ripe (late-harvested) grapes, or naturally sweet ones such as Muscat.

Light or full-bodied?

This is mainly an issue that affects red wines – with whites it's more a question of which grape variety you use, and whether you age the wine in oak. With reds, the winemaker also has the choice of leaving the wine in contact with the skins after fermentation in order to give it more body and structure.

Above: Grapes are handled quickly and hygienically so that wines taste clean and fresh.

Above: In recent years winemaking has been brought dramatically up-to-date in southern France. This re-equipped winery is at La Liquière, Hérault (AC Faugères).

Filtered or unfiltered?

The point of filtering is to get rid of any particles that remain in the wine that might make it unstable. Unfortunately, this can also strip out flavor and make the wine taste rather bland. Most winemakers play it safe and filter to avoid any risk of the wine being spoiled by rogue bacteria, but a few prefer to leave their wines unfiltered to give them more character.

Winemaker's jargon

Malolactic fermentation

"Malo" for short. A second fermentation that changes the sharp malic acid in wine into softer lactic acid. Near-automatic in reds but selectively used in whites (especially Chardonnays) to give them a fuller, fatter flavor.

Carbonic maceration

Instead of being crushed, the grapes are packed together under a layer of gas (CO_2) until they start to ferment. Used to give particularly bright, fruity flavors to light unoaked wines, such as Beaujolais.

Lees contact

The wine is left in contact with its lees (the residue left over from the yeast after fermentation). Used to give a creamy texture to more expensive Chardonnays and enrich the flavor of dry whites such as Muscadet (hence the expression *sur lie*).

The use of oak

Ageing wine in an oak barrel automatically increases its cost, so why do winemakers do it? Originally, it was the most practical method of storage, but these days, with stainless steel tanks, that's no longer necessary. What oak does contribute, however, are more interesting, complex flavors and the ability – particularly important in fine reds – to age.

Putting a wine in a barrel doesn't necessarily make it taste oaky, though. A winemaker can get different effects by using different kinds of wood.

Above: Oak barrels are charred (burned) to different extents and this has a huge influence on the flavor of the wine. The more charred the barrel, the more toasty the wine.

Old oak or new oak?

Wine that's put in a brand-new barrel will have much more obvious oaky flavors than wine that's aged in older ones, particularly if the new barrels are heavily toasted (new barrels are charred on the inside). In more expensive wines, winemakers will age different batches of wine in barrels of varying ages to get more complex effects. In time, the effect of old barrels is completely neutral – they just enable the wine to "breathe" more freely than inert stainless steel.

Big or small barrels?

The smaller the barrel, the oakier the effect. Wine aged in a standard 225-litre barrel will pick up oak flavors more quickly than one aged in a huge oak cask.

French or American oak?

Close-grained French oak is generally regarded as having more subtle, less strident flavors than American oak, but the dividing line between the two is less clear cut than it used to be. Most winemakers still choose French oak for their top whites, but the rich vanilla flavor of American oak suits robust reds such as Rioja and Australian Shiraz.

The other important factor that determines how oaky a wine tastes is how long it is left in oak. Lighter whites, such as Chardonnay, will only tend to get four to six months, whereas a full-bodied red might well spend up to two years in barrel. How oaky the wine seems after that depends on how soon you drink it. Very oaky reds and

whites are designed to be kept for a while before they're sold, to allow time for the fruit and oak to integrate. In an older wine you may not notice any obvious oak flavor at all – just a mellow smoothness.

Barrel fermentation

A technique frequently used for top Chardonnays. If the wine is fermented in barrel (rather than in stainless steel which is usually the case) the oak effect is more subtle.

Chips with everything

A lot of cheap, oaked wines aren't aged in barrels at all but have oak chips or staves added to the tank during

Above: Large oak vats are still being used for fermentation at Château Margaux in Bordeaux. They impart very little oak flavor compared with smaller barrels (*barriques*), which offer the wine much greater exposure to the oak.

fermentation. There's nothing wrong with that, so long as the wine doesn't end up tasting of wood shavings. Nevertheless, the practice is banned in more traditional wine-producing countries such as France. Even New World producers can be cagey about oak chips, referring to "oak influence" or "oak character." But the truth is that chips do give an oaky flavor without making the wine too expensive.

Wood words

If producers do use expensive oak barrels, they like to boast about it on the label as it obviously helps to justify the cost of the wine. Look for descriptions such as "barrel fermented," "barrel matured" and "barrel" or "barrique aged" (*élevé en fûts de chêne* in French). Barrel fermented wines (particularly Chardonnay) tend to give more subtle, sophisticated flavors than barrel matured ones, which are simply transferred to barrels after fermentation.

Tasting oak

Here are two very different examples of the impact oak can have on a wine. The two left-hand glasses show how the character of the Chardonnay grape completely changes depending on whether it is oaked or unoaked. (Being a fairly neutral grape variety it picks up much of its character from the barrels it is aged in.) On the right you can see how extended oak ageing produces an entirely different and more mature style of Cabernet Sauvignon than one which might have simply undergone contact with a few oak chips in a stainless steel tank.

Unoaked or Unwooded Chardonnay

An increasingly popular and easy-drinking style of Chardonnay.
Color: Light straw.
Aroma: With no oak to get in the way you can just focus on the natural fruit aromas of the wine – apple, citrus and peach.
Taste: A very fruity style of Chardonnay. You may pick up a hint of butteriness if the wine has gone through a malolactic fermentation (*see* pages 80–1), a process designed to make it taste smooth rather than sharp.

Conclusion: The use of the term "unoaked" on the label is designed to flag the fact that this is a particularly light, fresh style of Chardonnay, that you could drink as happily before a meal as with it.
Similar wines: Some wines (such as Chablis) are unoaked but don't make a feature of it on the front label. Check the label on the back of the bottle for references to stainless steel rather than oak barrels.

Californian Reserve Chardonnay

"Reserve" indicates a wine that's been aged in oak. California has the most full-bodied examples.
Color: Much deeper than the unoaked wine.
Aroma: You can immediately pick up aromas that are associated with oak rather than fruit – caramel, butterscotch, vanilla and toast.
Taste: It's not simply the complex flavors of the wine you notice (ripe, tropical, fruit flavors have now joined the butterscotch and caramel ones), but the rich, opulent texture.

Note the lingering aftertaste once you have swallowed.
Conclusion: This wine needs both food and time. Reserve wines are expensive, so save for special occasions and equally rich dishes. Unlike the unoaked Chardonnay it will improve with age.
Similar wines: Top French burgundies tend to be lighter and creamier, Australian Reserve Chardonnays fruitier. But at this kind of price level, the style of the wine depends very much on the individual approach of the winemaker.

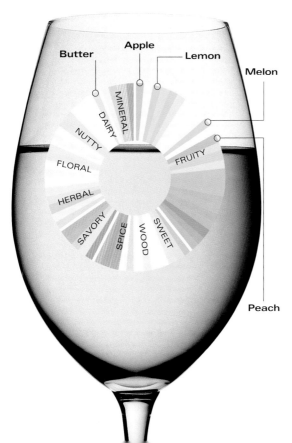

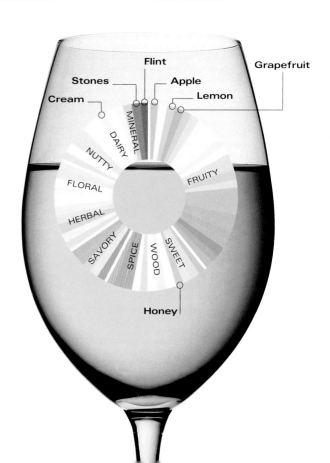

Oak flavor guide

VANILLA
The vanilla flavor
you pick up in wines
such as Chardonnay
generally indicates
the wine has been aged
in new oak barrels.

TOAST
Barrels that have
been heavily charred
inside can make
a wine taste almost
toasty and leave
a spicy aftertaste.

CEDAR
The effect of long
ageing in barrels
creates a soft, mellow
flavor, more like
cedar (or even tobacco)
than oak.

Bulgarian Special Reserve Cabernet Sauvignon

A wine that might have spent at least one and up to three years in oak, and which may well be five years old before it hits the shelf.

Color: Garnet red. Beginning to fade at the edges as older wines do.

Aroma: Dried, rather than fresh, fruit aromas. Preserved plums, raisins, dried cherries and perhaps a whiff of cinnamon spice.

Taste: A sweet, delicate, dried fruit flavor, combined with a slight sharpness – a bit like sun-dried cherries. There's no trace of the normal blackcurrant flavor associated with Cabernet.

Conclusion: The long oak ageing, probably in old barrels or casks, has integrated the fruit and the oak. You wouldn't describe it as fruity and, but for a slight trace of cedary spice, you can't really pick out the oak.

Similar wines: Few countries can deliver such a well-integrated, mature wine at the lower end of the price level for Cabernet Sauvignon. Valdepeñas in Spain and Copertino in southern Italy come closest. What you're getting, in effect, is a cut-price claret.

Oaked South African Cabernet Sauvignon

Inexpensive South African Cabernet Sauvignons frequently have a few oak chips added to round them out.

Color: Light, ruby red.

Aroma: Much more obvious than the Bulgarian Cabernet. Sweet blackcurrant, plum and blackberry fruit, mingling with touches of toasty oak.

Taste: An altogether smoother, fruitier, plummier wine. In spite of being exposed to oak for a much shorter time, the oak influence is more obvious, leaving you with a distinct, spicy aftertaste.

Conclusion: A similar alcohol content and price to the Bulgarian Cabernet, but there the resemblance ends. This is a much younger wine, for immediate consumption, and likely to appeal far more to people who enjoy wines from the New World.

Similar wines: Cabernet from the Languedoc region of France. Other New World Cabernets (e.g. from Australia and Chile) tend to be lusher, riper and sweeter, but may also owe their oak character to chips rather than barrels.

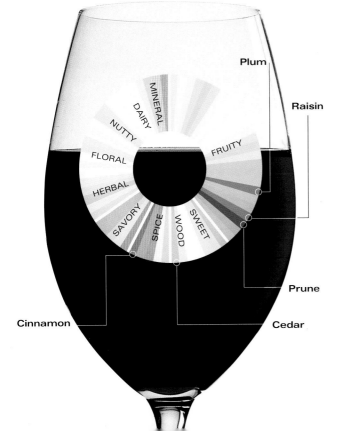

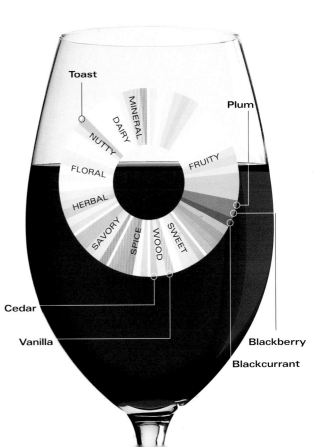

Ageing and vintages

There are two reasons to age a wine. The first is that it might be the only chance you have to buy the wine at an affordable price. If you let someone else – the producer or the wine merchant – do the ageing for you and buy the wine when it's ready to drink, you'll pay more. (This is assuming you can even get hold of it. Many of the best wines are in limited supply.)

The second is that a wine is not yet ready to drink. This tends to apply mainly to more expensive wines – aromatic whites which have not developed their "true" character, or powerful reds that need time to mellow out and soften – not to the vast majority of modern wines. Whether you think this is worthwhile depends on whether you like the more complex flavors of older wine. Many people do not.

It's also only worth ageing wine if you have the right kind of storage facilities (*see* page 44). If yours are less than ideal, get a reputable merchant to arrange storage for you.

Wines that age well
The following wines are worth keeping for considerably longer than the minimum periods suggested on page 44. (Bear in mind that the size of bottle the wine is in makes a difference to how long it will keep. A half bottle won't last as long as a standard (75cl) bottle. A magnum will last longer.

White wines
Good-quality white burgundy such as Chablis and other top Chardonnays. Aromatic wines such as Riesling, Gewürztraminer and Pinot Gris (particularly those from Alsace and Germany), Australian Semillon and white Bordeaux. Wines from the Marsanne grape also age well.

Red wines
Moderate to expensive wines from Bordeaux, Burgundy and the Rhône. Top Italian and Spanish reds. Full-bodied New World reds such as Californian and Australian Cabernet and Australian Shiraz.

(Good sources of relatively inexpensive mature reds are Spain, southern Italy and Bulgaria.)

Dessert, fortified and sparkling wines
Sauternes, top quality Vouvray and other sweet wines from the Loire; Rieslings from Germany, Alsace, Austria and New Zealand. Vintage and older tawny ports. Madeira. Vintage Champagne.

Signs of ageing
The most obvious sign of ageing is the color of the wine. Red wines get paler and white wines become deeper and more golden as they age. You can also tell from the aroma, which is more complex and less obviously fruity in aged wines. Finally, the feel of a mature wine in your mouth is generally softer and sweeter than that of a young wine.

Does vintage matter?
A lot of people worry about their lack of knowledge of vintages, but for the

vast majority of modern wines, particularly those from the New World, the vintage (i.e. the year the grapes were harvested) doesn't actually matter that much. Modern techniques enable winemakers to do a decent job, even in the most adverse conditions. The worst thing that can happen in a bad year is that there isn't so much wine available and that it won't keep for as long.

It's only when you start looking at more expensive wines, produced in cooler, northerly regions, such as

Bordeaux and Burgundy, that it matters whether it was a good or bad vintage (i.e. whether the grapes were able to ripen successfully or were blighted by bad weather). Obviously that differs from one region to another. An unsuccessful vintage in Bordeaux doesn't necessarily mean a bad one in Burgundy.

Vintages also have more significance with wines such as port and Champagne where vintages are "declared" (i.e. the producers claim

it's a particularly good year). Even then, I wouldn't worry about trying to bone up on them. If this is going to affect the type of wine you buy – invest in an annual wine guide, or consult a specialist merchant for specific advice.

When working out how old a bottle of wine is, remember that countries in the southern hemisphere such as Australia harvest their grapes six months ahead of those in Europe and North America.

Above: This line-up of some of the greatest vintages of the century shows just how long great wines can last. Amazingly, even a bottle as old as the 1921 Château d'Yquem would still be drinkable, though for many collectors, the buzz is more about owning a wine this rare, than the actual taste. Wines like this would only be available at auction or in private cellars and would cost a small fortune to buy. However, it does underline that wine of this caliber can be a good investment for the future.

Where wine is made

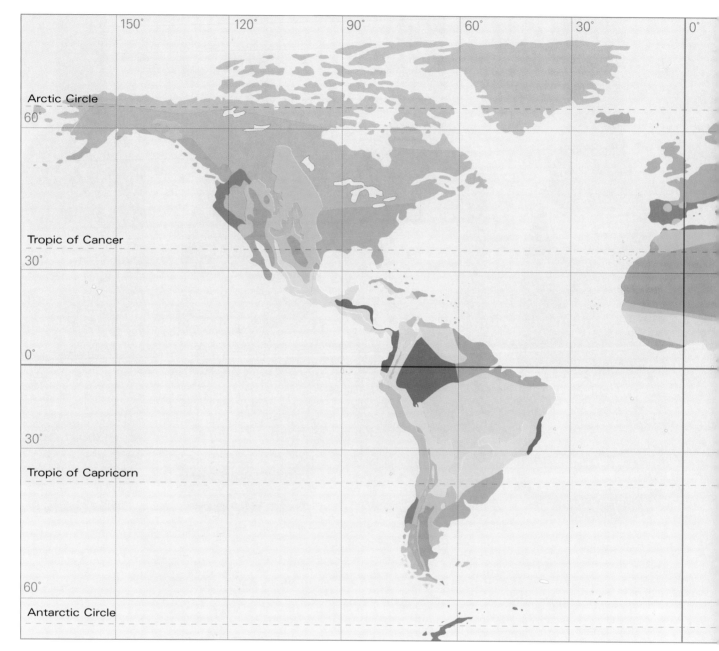

If you look at a map of the world, remarkably few areas are suitable for grape growing. By and large, vineyards are concentrated in the temparate (green) areas to the south of the Tropic of Capricorn and to the north of the Tropic of Cancer, but even these regions contain areas that are too cold to grow grapes on a commercial basis (Scotland and Scandinavia, for example). Areas that are near the sea tend to have more moderate climates than those that are landlocked. For example, it is possible to grow grapes successfully on the West Coast or eastern seaboard of the United States, but much more difficult in the center where temperatures are more extreme. What vines dislike, though, is heat combined with humidity – the climate you get around the equator. This disrupts their natural growing cycle and makes them more prone to disease.

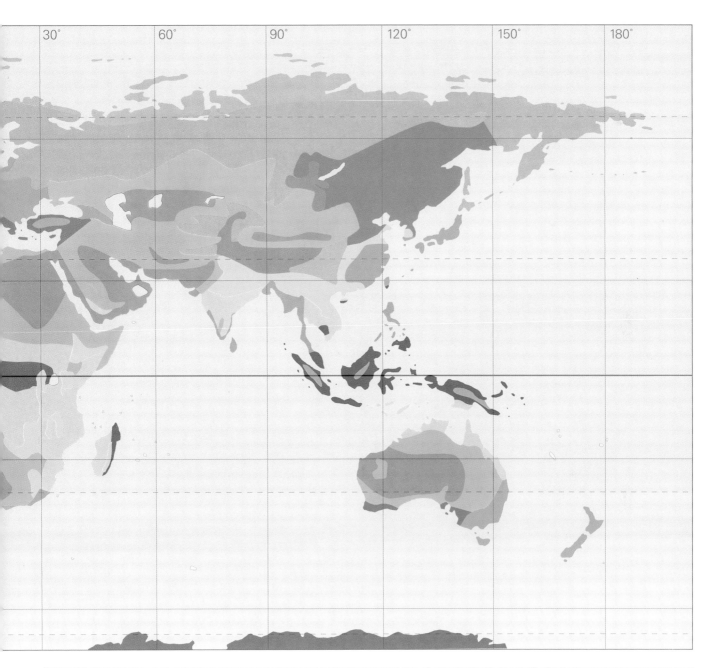

Key to climatic regions

Rain forest *(tropical)*

Monsoon *(tropical)*

Savannah *(tropical)*

Steppe *(dry)*

Desert *(dry)*

Dry winter *(warm temperate rainy)*

Dry summer *(warm temperate rainy)*

No dry season *(warm temperate rainy)*

Dry winter *(cold temperate rainy)*

No dry season *(cold temperate rainy)*

Tundra *(polar)*

Polar *(polar)*

France

Nobody does it quite like France. Its wine regions are the most varied, its wines still the benchmark by which almost every other wine is judged. It has, in Bordeaux and Burgundy, what are still universally acclaimed, the world's best reds, in Burgundy the finest most opulent whites, in Champagne the greatest sparkling wine and in Sauternes the most prized sweet wine. Yet, it also has the worst wines. How many disappointing experiences have you had with French wine? More, I bet, than with any other country.

Sorting the sheep from the goats is a hard task, but there are four key factors which should give you some kind of clue to how good the wine is.

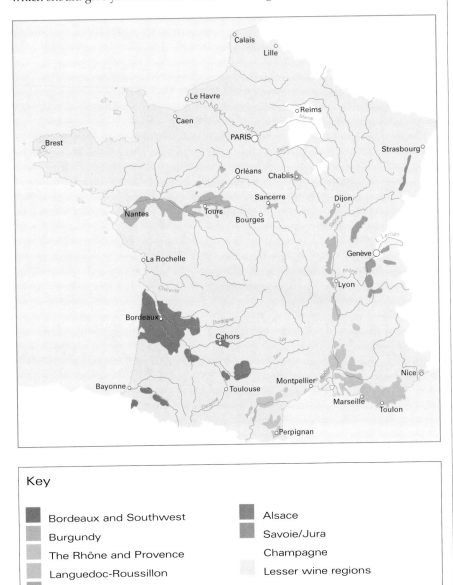

Key

- Bordeaux and Southwest
- Burgundy
- The Rhône and Provence
- Languedoc-Roussillon
- The Loire
- Alsace
- Savoie/Jura
- Champagne
- Lesser wine regions

Class of wine

French wine is divided into four main categories:

Vin de table – as the name suggests, basic table wine.

Vin de pays – literally "country wines" (i.e. wines that are typical of the area they come from). This is an important category accounting for about a quarter of all French wines. Not bound by the strict rules that apply to AC wines (*see* below) and generally excellent value.

VDQS (Vin Délimité de Qualité Supérieure) – an increasingly irrelevant category one step down from AC.

Appellation Contrôlée – wines labeled AC or AOC are subject to a strict set of rules that govern which grape varieties can be planted, how many grapes each vine may produce and how the wine that comes from them should be made. It generally means the wine will be typical of its region, but doesn't actually guarantee quality.

What part of the region the wine comes from

Basically, some appellations are better than others. For example, Muscadet de Sèvre-et-Maine is better than basic Muscadet, and Hermitage than Crozes-Hermitage. The more specific an area is in terms of being limited to a village or even a single vineyard, the better the wine is likely to be. (The word *villages*, in fact, is generally reassuring. Beaujolais-Villages is better than basic Beaujolais.)

You may also see the words *Premier Cru* or *Grand Cru* on a label, particularly on wines from Burgundy. That means the wine has come from vineyards which have been officially recognized as superior in quality – though it may not, in fact, be as good as that the description *Premier Cru* (first growth) might suggest.

Another word to look for is *Côtes* – an indication that the wine comes from grapes planted on slopes, better-quality land than vineyards that are planted on the flat, as slopes are more exposed to the sun. *Supérieur,* on the other hand, doesn't mean superior, rather that the wine is required to have a slightly higher minimum level of alcohol.

Quality of the producer

The most reliable guarantee of quality in France is usually that the wine comes from a good producer. The best way to find that out who the good producers are is from a specialist wine merchant, or through current wine guides. The indication that the wine comes from an independent producer is the words *mis en bouteille au château* or *domaine*, which mean that the wine has been bottled at the owner's estate.

Some wines, particularly in traditional areas such as Bordeaux and Burgundy, are produced by *négociants* – dealers who buy grapes and juice, make wine from them and market it; some also grow their own grapes. Standards of *négociants* vary (some make very good wine, some are less inspiring). Other wines are made by cooperatives (co-ops) – organizations run for the benefit of local growers who sell them their grapes to make into wine. Co-op wines used to be very basic, but these days can represent excellent value for your money.

Above: The classic image of French wine production – a serene château with vineyards.

How good the vintage is

Vintages are important in France – where many regions, including the Loire, Bordeaux and Burgundy, are at the limits of the kind of climate in which grape growing is viable. People sometimes talk as if a year is good or bad for the whole of France, but (other than in exceptional years like 1990 – an excellent vintage all around) – the weather does vary (sometimes dramatically) from region to region.

This doesn't matter quite so much for inexpensive wines, as many of the worst effects of a poor vintage can be overcome these days by modern winemaking techniques. It is worth checking with a specialist, or in a wine guide, if you are buying wines to lay down or keep.

Bordeaux and the Southwest

Lafite, Latour, Mouton-Rothschild – Bordeaux boasts the best-known names in the wine world. Yet that shouldn't lead you to think its wines are all expensive. The so-called First Growths are just a fraction of the wines this vast growing region produces, and that's not even counting the white, rosé and dessert wines that also bear the Bordeaux name.

Red Bordeaux

Red Bordeaux is generally a blend of Cabernet Sauvignon and Merlot, but may also include other grapes such as Cabernet Franc, Malbec and Petit Verdot. What style of wine results depends on which grape predominates. Cabernet typically produces more austere, elegant, dry reds than Merlot, which is softer and fruitier (*see* opposite and pages 66–9).

Most Bordeaux reds are straightforward Bordeaux or Bordeaux Supérieur, which means they can be blended from grapes grown anywhere in the region. If the label mentions a district such as Médoc or Graves, then the wine is likely to be of higher quality, still more so if it's the best area within that district, such as Haut-Médoc or Pessac-Léognan.

The next step up are wines from specific villages or communes. The Haut-Médoc has four famous ones – Margaux, St-Julien, Pauillac and St-Estèphe. St-Emilion is surrounded by a cluster of top quality villages such as Montagne-St-Emilion and Lussac-St-Emilion. In between is the important Graves region, to the south of Bordeaux.

On top of this the Médoc has its own classification system, which was drawn up in 1855 and ranks the properties (*châteaux*) of the area into five groups. These are called *Crus Classés* or Classed Growths, the most famous of which are First Growths such as Châteaux Lafite, Mouton-Rothschild and Latour. Below that – and representing some of the best value in Bordeaux – are wines that are labeled *Cru Bourgeois*.

You may also hear the term *petits châteaux* – wines from modest properties that are not officially rated. Similarly, "second" wines – wines from major *châteaux* that have failed to meet the exacting standards of the top growths – can offer far better value than their more famous counterparts.

In fact, the reassuring thing about Bordeaux is that you don't need to go for well-known names to drink well. Indeed, the way that prices have soared over the past few years, you'll do your pocketbook a favor if you don't. A producer will always be able to put a premium on a wine labeled St-Emilion, for example; far less so on

Below: Monbazillac and Bergerac offer good alternatives to Bordeaux.

a wine labeled Fronsac, Canon-Fronsac or Côtes de Castillon, which come from just over the border. Other modestly priced Bordeaux appellations to look for are Côtes de Bourg and Côtes de Francs.

Rosé

Given the huge amounts of red wine being made, it's hardly surprising that some of the juice is run off as rosé. Bordeaux rosé, these days, tends to be attractively fragrant and fruity – more elegant than the traditional *clairet*, which was almost a light red.

White Bordeaux

Dry, white Bordeaux has much less of a reputation than either red or sweet Bordeaux, but undeservedly so. The main grape is Sauvignon, which is either made in a simple, crisp, citrussy style, as in Bordeaux Blanc and Entre-Deux-Mers, or blended with Sémillon and lightly oaked, which produces lusher, smoother wines. The best wines come from Péssac-Leognan, the most prestigious part of the Graves region, and can last for many years.

The sweet wines of the region tend to be eclipsed by the fabled wines of Sauternes and Barsac (*see* pages 20–1) but there are many lesser-known wines such as Cadillac, Loupiac, Ste-Croix-du-Mont and Monbazillac (just outside Bordeaux) that are made in a similar style and are much more affordable.

Southwest France

This is a huge area that covers much of the western side of the country from the Dordogne down to the Spanish

Reading Bordeaux labels

The vast majority of labels on bottles from the Bordeaux region look very similar. They tend to be traditional, with rather grand lettering, and often show a picture of the château. It is the classic image of high-class French wine. These two labels are from very different wines. The first is from one of the very finest St-Emilion châteaux, Cheval Blanc, which has an unusually high proportion of the Cabernet Franc grape (60 percent, the rest made up of Merlot which usually dominates here). The second label is from the left bank of the Gironde, specifically from Listrac-Médoc, a commune offering great value for the money compared with its glamorous, more illustrious neighbors in the Haut-Médoc.

① **Château Cheval Blanc** the name of the property
② **1981** the vintage (a very good one in St-Emilion)
③ **St-Emilion** the commune
④ **1er Grand Cru Classé** the classification (the very highest rank for St-Emilion, the others in descending order are Grand Cru Classé and Grand Cru).
⑤ **Appellation Saint-Emilion 1er Grand Cru Classé Contrôlée** the official classification
⑥ **Mis en bouteille au château** bottled at the château
⑦ **Produce of France**
⑧ **Sté Civile du Cheval Blanc, Htiers Fourcaud-Laussac Propriétaires à St-Emilion (Gironde) France** full details of the producer/owner
⑨ **75cl** the size of the bottle

① **1988** the vintage (very good for the Médoc)
② **Château Saransot-Dupré** the name of the property
③ **Listrac-Médoc** the commune
④ **Appellation Listrac-Médoc Contrôlée** the official description of the appellation
⑤ **12.5%** the alcoholic strength
⑥ **Cru Bourgeois** the classification (The Médoc classifications are led by the Crus Classés – the First, Second, Third, Fourth and Fifth Growths – the First Growths still fit the description, but the ranking for the rest is more questionable. Grand Bourgeois comes next, followed by Cru Bourgeois. These final two are not nearly as lowly as they seem.)
⑦ **750ml** the size of the bottle
⑧ **Yves Ramond Propriétaire à Listrac-Médoc, 33480 – France** name and address of the owner
⑨ **Mis en bouteille au château** bottled at the château
⑩ **Produce of France**

border. The wines in the immediate neighborhood of Bordeaux – Bergerac, Buzet, Côtes de Duras and Côtes du Marmandais – are very similar to (and often better value for money than) Bordeaux, otherwise, there's no clear pattern. You find some attractively crisp, inexpensive whites under the Vin de Pays des Côtes de

Gascogne label and some highly individual, full-bodied reds from appellations such as Cahors and Madiran.

Some of France's quirkiest and most interesting dry and sweet wines also come from this area, from Jurançon right down at the foothills of the Pyrenees.

Burgundy

There's no getting away from it, Burgundy is maddeningly difficult. On the one hand it offers some of the most sublime drinking on the planet. On the other, it is capable of producing wines so downright dull it makes you wonder what all the fuss is about. Given that it's also extraordinarily difficult to remember the many different names of the wines in the region, it's no surprise that people give up in despair.

The easiest starting point is the grape varieties. Almost all whites are made from Chardonnay (apart from the few that are made from the less exciting Aligoté grape) and the reds from Pinot Noir or Gamay. They get their distinctive character from the fact that the region is comparatively northerly (Chablis is on a similar latitude to the Loire), and has a variable climate that results in considerable variations in quality from one year to the next. And, by and large, winemaking methods are still quite traditional, resulting in subtler, less obviously fruity wines than those of the New World.

The area is divided into five main regions, two of which, Chablis and Beaujolais, are not really thought of as Burgundy. The others are the Côte d'Or, the Côte Chalonnaise and the Mâconnais. The area wine-lovers really get excited about is the Cote d'Or, a 30-mile-long strip of land to the south of Dijon, that produces all of Burgundy's greatest and most famous wines. The northern half is called the Côte de Nuits and produces mainly reds; the southern half, the Côte de Beaune, produces the greatest whites, as well as some fine reds.

More familiar are the names of individual villages or communes, such

Reading Burgundy labels

If you look at these two burgundy labels, you can get a feel for what the wines are like. The Bourgogne (on the right) is made from grapes that could come from anywhere in the region and is a comparatively affordable wine (but in this case could offer considerable value for money as it is made by a grower in Meursault – a village renowned for its high-quality wines). The Musigny (on the left) is a grand, highly-prized wine from a top producer, made with grapes from a tiny specified area and is consequently expensively priced.

① **Musigny** the name of the vineyard
② **Grand Cru** status (in this case, the highest rank in Burgundy)
③ **Appellation Musigny Contrôlée** classification (being a Grand Cru, it is, in fact, a mini appellation)
④ **Cuvée Vieilles Vignes** a name the producer has given the wine indicating that it is from old vines
⑤ **Domaine Comte Georges de Vogüé** the name of the producer (a famous one)
⑥ **Chambolle-Musigny (Côte d'Or)** where the producer is based
⑦ **Réserve numérottée** this tells us it's a numbered bottle (i.e. only a very small quantity was made)
⑧ **Mis en bouteilles au domaine** bottled at the domaine – the producer's commercial details are given
⑨ **1989** the vintage (a great one)

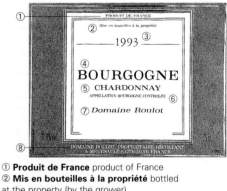

① **Produit de France** product of France
② **Mis en bouteilles à la propriété** bottled at the property (by the grower)
③ **1993** the vintage (a good one)
④ **Bourgogne** Burgundy, the area the grapes come from (could be from anywhere in the region)
⑤ **Chardonnay** the grape variety it is made from (normally not stated and only appears on the label at this lowest classification level)
⑥ **Appellation Bourgogne Contrôlée** classification
⑦ **Domaine Roulot** the name of the producer
⑧ **Domaine Roulot, propriétaire-recoltant à Meursault (Côte d'Or), France** the producer's full name and address

as Meursault, Gevrey-Chambertin and Nuits-St-Georges. Each area is subdivided into individual vineyards, which may in turn be divided among many different owners. The best vineyards (or theoretically the best) are designated *Premier Cru* or *Grand Cru*, though *Premier Cru* (the less important of the two) can be hugely variable. At the bottom of the pyramid are wines that are labeled after the district they come from, such as Mâcon Blanc, or after the region as a whole, which are just called Bourgogne.

White burgundy

White burgundy is regarded as the benchmark for Chardonnay but, in fact, there is a marked difference between the severe, steely style of Chablis, a rich, buttery Meursault and the delicate cream-and-hazelnut character of a Puligny- or Chassagne-Montrachet. Most of these differences don't come into play, however, until you start looking at more expensive wines or ones that are two or three years old.

Less well-known white burgundies, that offer good value, include Auxey-Duresses, Mâcon-Villages, Montagny, Pernand-Vergelesses, Rully, St-Aubin and St-Véran.

Red burgundy

Red burgundy has a fine, silky feel in the mouth that makes it one of the most sensuous, as well as one of the most delicious, wines around. Younger, less expensive wines, such as basic Bourgogne Rouge, have a particularly pure, soft, raspberry fruit.

The more expensive appellations are more intensely plummy and

Above: Autumnal vineyard by the château at Gervrey-Chambertin in the Côte de Nuits.

exotic, fading over time to a truffley complexity. Highly prized red burgundies include Chambolle-Musigny, Gevrey-Chambertin, Nuits-St-Georges and Vosne-Romanée.

For good value wines try Chorey-lès-Beaune, Savigny-lès-Beaune, Fixin, Givry, Marsannay, Mercurey, Hautes-Côtes de Beaune and Hautes-Côtes de Nuits.

Beaujolais

Beaujolais is lumped together with Burgundy because it is in virtually the same area. Despite the similarities with the lighter styles of Pinot Noir, the region is taken far less seriously thanks (or, rather, no thanks) to the essentially frivolous Beaujolais Nouveau. The two main distinguishing features in Beaujolais are the grape the wine is made from – Gamay – and a technique called carbonic maceration, a method of fermenting grapes that results in very fresh, vivid cherry-flavored fruit.

Although most people probably think of Beaujolais as a simple, light red wine, there are, in fact, more substantial, weighty *cru* Beaujolais. Brouilly, Chénas, Chiroubles, Fleurie, Juliénas, Morgon, Moulin-à-Vent, Régnié, St-Amour and Côte de Brouilly – many of them named after individual villages. A small amount of white Beaujolais is also produced.

The Rhône and Provence

In spite of possessing some of the oldest vineyards in France, the Rhône oddly doesn't have the same prestige as Bordeaux and Burgundy, but for lovers of full-bodied wines its rich, sun-baked reds take a lot of beating.

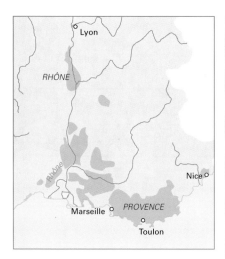

Rhône reds

This region runs down the Rhône Valley from Lyon to Avignon and divides into two distinct parts. The northern Rhône, with its precipitous rocky slopes, is the smaller area and produces what are still considered to be the greatest Syrah wines in the world (the variety is believed to have been first introduced by the Greeks). The most expensive are Hermitage (the inspiration for Australian Shiraz) and Cornas, both dense, brooding wines that need at least five and often ten years to be at their best, and the immensely fashionable Côte-Rôtie (*see* right). Cheaper options are St-Joseph (*see* page 74) and Crozes-Hermitage, which is lighter, but still exhibits Syrah's spicy, peppery character. Further south the pattern changes. Grenache joins Syrah as the dominant grape and the wines are lighter and more approachable. The exception is the rich, full-bodied

Châteauneuf-du-Pape – a wine distinguished for two things: the papal coat of arms embossed on the bottle and the fact that it can include up to 13 different grape varieties in its blend. Other interesting southern Rhône wines that are often overlooked are Lirac, Gigondas and Vacqueyras – warm, sweet, spicy, generous reds that make good all-purpose drinking.

Well over half the wines from the region, however, are basic Côtes du Rhône and simple *vin de pays*, most notably from the Côtes du Ventoux. The ones to watch, however, are the up-and-coming areas of Costières de Nîmes (which produces particularly robust, smoky reds), Coteaux de l'Ardèche and Coteaux du Tricastin, which are producing some of the region's most innovative wines.

Rhône whites

Only four percent of the wines produced in the Rhône are white, and they generally don't come cheap. Like the reds they are made from local grape varieties, principally Marsanne and Roussanne, and tend to have quite a rustic, earthy quality that is more

Above: La Chapelle is one of the finest Hermitage vineyards, overlooking the River Rhône.

Above: Rousset with Montagne Ste. Victoire beyond, Bouches-du-Rhône.

popular among enthusiasts than newcomers to wine. The exception is the cult wine Condrieu, a rare, exotically scented white that is made from the Viognier grape and regarded as the benchmark for Viognier wines everywhere else in the world.

Rhône sweet wines

Amid all that sea of red, there are two sweet wines that stand out. Clairette de Die, a fragrant, honeysuckle-scented sparkling wine (the best wines are labeled "Tradition") and the deliciously grapey Muscat de Beaumes-de-Venise.

Provence

It's hardly surprising that wines from Provence should be expensive when you think of land prices in this chic part of France, but they are stylish. The ones you're most likely to see are rosés (though one of the best-known rosés, Tavel, in fact, comes from the Rhône). There are a few crisp whites from boutique wineries in tiny appellations such as Bellet (up in the hills behind Nice), Cassis, Palette and Bandol, though the latter is best known for its robust, savory reds that are made from the tricky and temperamental Mourvèdre grape.

Less rarified options are wines labeled Côtes du Provence, Côtes du Lubéron, Coteaux d'Aix en Provence and Les Baux de Provence, though some of the region's best producers such as Domaines Ott and Domaine du Trévallon also (confusingly) use some of these appellations for their top wines.

Reading Rhône labels

The Rhône Valley is a very large area, so the key to reading the label is to work out just where in the region the wine comes from. As with Burgundy, the less well-known the area the wine comes from, the better the value is likely to be. A wine that comes from a specific vineyard or famous village will be a lot more sought-after and consequently expensive.

① **Domaine de l'Ameillaud** name of the property
② **1996** year of vintage
③ **Cairanne** A named village within the Côtes du Rhône appellation (an indication of quality)
④ **Côtes du Rhône Villages** - appellation
⑤ **Appellation Côtes du Rhône Villages Contrôlée** official classification
⑥ **Produce of France**
⑦ **Mis en bouteille au Domaine de l'Ameillaud** bottled at the Domaine de l'Ameillaud
⑧ **Cairanne 84290 France** address
⑨ **Alc 13% by vol** - alcoholic strength (quite high for a Côtes du Rhône)
⑩ **Net contents 375ml** half-bottle size

① **La Turque** name of vineyard (the producer can use this name as the company has registered it officially; in the Rhône, the best vineyards do not have their own individual classifications as they do in Burgundy and Alsace)
② **Côte Brune** along with the Côte Blonde, the core of the Côte-Rôtie appellation
③ **Côte-Rôtie** appellation (one of the most sought-after in the Rhône)
④ **Appellation Côte-Rôtie Contrôlée** official classification
⑤ **Récolté, vinifié, élevé et mis en bouteille par** harvested, vinified, matured and bottled by E Guigal (one of the most famous producers in the Rhône)
⑥ **Ampuis (Rhône) France** address
⑦ **13% vol** alcoholic strength
⑧ **Produit de France** product of France
⑨ **75cl** size of bottle

Languedoc-Roussillon

In a way, the Languedoc (the Midi) represents the wine world in a microcosm. Old sits alongside new, gnarled old growers beside keen young Australian winemakers, shabby dilapidated cellars next to gleaming stainless steel – the region exploits almost every grape variety and winemaking technique in the book. It's the dynamic heartland of France – a laboratory where winemakers, hemmed in by restrictions elsewhere, can come to experiment.

This area is huge. It stretches across half of the south of France, from Nîmes right down to the Spanish border. It is hot, and that makes it mainly red wine country, but modern technology has enabled it to produce fresh, fruity whites as well.

The sheer variety of wine it produces is confusing, but it basically divides into those who make their wines by the rules (the traditional appellations) and those who do not (the *vins de pays*). Following are the main types of wine that you'll find.

Modern varietals

Many of the Languedoc's wines are produced and marketed as a single grape variety, as they would be in Australia or California. This is done as much by French companies, such as Skalli (Fortant de France) and Val d'Orbieu, as Australian companies such as BRL Hardy. The flavors are those of New World wines. The labels – which usually carry the description Vin de Pays d'Oc – are slick and contemporary. The region has proved particularly successful for Chardonnay,* Cabernet and Merlot, and is increasingly promising for Viognier and Syrah.

(*Though one of the best Chardonnays is an* appellation contrôlée *Chardonnay, Limoux, from the north of the region.*)

Traditional reds

The area's traditional reds are based on the same grapes as the Rhône (Syrah, Grenache and Mourvèdre), but are often blended with less distinguished varieties, such as Cinsault and Carignan, which tend to make them slightly less graceful.

The biggest appellation by far is Corbières, noted for its mature, oak-aged reds. The wines of St-Chinian, Fitou and Collioure in Roussillon tend to be robust and concentrated; those of Minervois and Faugères, more sensuous and supple, though the style does vary between one producer and another, depending on how traditional they are in their winemaking methods. (Whether, for instance, they use new oak barrels, old wooden casks or even concrete tanks, as is quite common in

Above: This is the traditional way of growing vines in the Languedoc – as small bushes.

the region.) There are also a lot of light, inexpensive reds, such as Côtes du Roussillon, many of which come from co-ops – organizations that play an important part in the Midi. Although at one stage they simply produced wine in bulk (and still do for the locals, of whom I'm happy to count myself!), they now offer a much more ambitious range of wines. They also give fantastic value for the money.

New-wave reds and whites

A growing number of wines in the Languedoc are produced by talented winemakers who work outside the official classification system, but still aim to produce distinctive wines from local grape varieties. Some, such as Mas de Daumas Gassac, simply describe their wines as *vins de pays*. Others use the catch-all title Coteaux du Languedoc, including up-and-coming areas such as La Clape, Montpeyroux and Pic St-Loup. In contrast with modern varietals, they tend to come from more than one grape variety.

The whites – largely made from Rhône varieties such as Marsanne, Roussanne and Viognier – are peachy and aromatic, the reds fruitier and more supple than those from the traditional appellations.

Traditional whites and rosés

White wine doesn't play much of a role in this part of France. As in Provence, they drink more rosé. Both tend to be fresh, crisp and dry – the whites from local grape varieties such as Chasan, Grenache Blanc, Maccabeo, Terret and Picpoul (a refreshing Muscadet-like white); the rosés from Cinsault, Grenache and Syrah.

Above: Dynamic modern winemaking at Skalli-Fortant de France, near Sète.

Sweet and fortified wines

There are two distinct styles of sweet wines: fragrant Muscats such as Muscat de Frontignan and Muscat de St-Jean de Minervois, which are similar in style (though often cheaper) than the Rhône's Muscat de Beaumes-de-Venise; and Roussillon's speciality – rich, warm, concentrated port-like reds made from Grenache. The names to look for are Banyuls, Maury and Rivesaltes.

The Loire, Alsace, Jura and Savoie

Although best known for its crisp, dry whites, the Loire is a versatile wine region that is also home to stylish reds, world-class sweet wines and good value sparklers. Well to the north of most major wine-producing regions, it covers a huge area from the Atlantic Coast inland to Burgundy, but the best wines are concentrated in the 300-odd miles between Nantes and Sancerre.

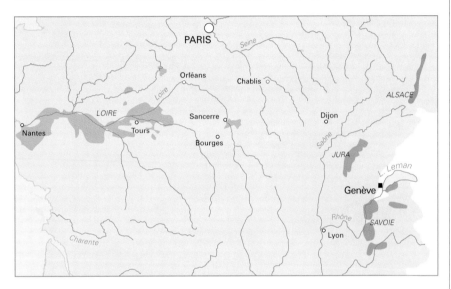

Loire white wines

Nearest to the sea is Muscadet de Sèvre-et-Maine – appropriately enough since the ultra crisp, dry, citrussy wines it produces are perfect with seafood. It's worth paying extra for the best-quality *sur lie*, wines which have an attractively nutty character (*see* page 81).

The Loire's most successful grape variety is Sauvignon Blanc, which achieves particularly fine, delicate, flint-like flavors from the limestone soil. Sancerre and Pouilly-Fumé (not to be confused with Pouilly-Fuissé, which is a white burgundy) are the benchmarks. You can often get better value, though, from lesser-known appellations such as Quincy, Reuilly, Menetou-Salon and Sauvignon de Touraine, which is sometimes referred to as "poor man's Sancerre."

The other widely planted grape is Chenin Blanc, which makes a wide range of styles from rather dull, acidic whites to amazingly long-lived, honeyed dessert wines, such as

Bonnezeaux and Quarts de Chaume. A number of wines, including Vouvray and Montlouis, come in varying degrees of sweetness – *sec* (dry), *demi-sec* (medium-dry) and *moelleux* (sweet) – so it's important to check which you're getting when you buy. A good starting point for the sweeter styles is the very reasonably priced Coteaux du Layon.

Although the Loire is principally a traditional region, there are some more modern whites being made, particularly as *vin de pays*. Chardonnay Vin de Pays du Jardin de la France in particular can be attractively light and citrussy.

Loire reds and rosés

Lacking the richness of more southerly wines, Loire reds are something of an acquired taste, but their lightness and elegance attracts a devoted following among wine enthusiasts. Names to look for are Bourgueil, Chinon and

Below: Steep, chalky vineyards near Sancerre – perfect for top Sauvignon Blanc.

Saumur-Champigny, which are made from Cabernet Franc, and red Sancerre, which comes from Pinot Noir. Gamay is also widely used to make light, Beaujolais-style reds. So far as rosé is concerned, Sancerre Rosé and Cabernet d'Anjou easily outclass the ubiquitous Rosé d'Anjou.

Alsace

If you look at a map of France, Alsace is even farther to the north than the Loire, yet because of its particularly favored microclimate, it's actually a lot warmer.

At first sight the wines seem more similar to those of Germany than of France. Indeed Alsace is home to many of the same aromatic grape varieties. But its wines are generally much riper and higher in alcohol than its neighbor's, with a rich, spicy character that often takes a year or two to develop.

Alsace wine terms

Like German wines, wines from Alsace come in different degrees of sweetness. If you see the words *vendange tardive* (late harvest) on a label, that generally indicates a sweeter style (though, occasionally they can be dry, just high in alcohol). Much less common is *séléction des grains nobles*, superb sweet wines that are only made when the grapes develop botrytis (*see* pages 20–1). The best wines (theoretically at least) come from single vineyards and may be labeled Grand Cru. As they tend to be very expensive, they're only worth buying if you're prepared to keep them the ten years or so they need to show at their best.

Above: Schlossberg, overlooking Kayserberg town, is one of Alsace's finest vineyards.

The wines are relatively easy to come to grips with because they're based on single-grape varieties (with the exception of Pinot Noir, Alsace is exclusively a white-wine producing region). The easiest introduction is to try a Pinot Blanc, which is light, dry and appley, a refreshingly floral Sylvaner, or even a straightforward Vin d'Alsace.

But the wine identified with Alsace more than any other is Gewurztraminer, an amazingly exotic wine that tastes of lychees, red roses and Turkish delight. The region's other serious whites are Riesling, Tokay-Pinot Gris (not to be confused with the famous Hungarian sweet wine Tokay (*see* page 119) and Muscat (rarer than the other three), all of which are made in dry and sweeter versions. None tend to come cheap, but they are a reliable choice on restaurant wine lists, particularly with the spicy flavors of Thai and southeast Asian cuisine.

Alsace also produces attractive, light, creamy sparkling wine, Crémant d'Alsace, as well as some spectacular fruit *eaux de vie* – beyond the scope of this book, but well worth trying.

Jura and Savoie

These are two wine-producing areas to the east of France that produce wines similar to their neighbors (Burgundy, in the case of the Jura; Switzerland, in the case of Savoie). Neither is exported in quantity. The Jura also produces a rare wine called Vin Jaune, an interesting curiosity that's a bit like dry sherry.

Champagne and other French sparkling wines

When you look at the map and see just how far to the north of France Champagne is, it seems a miracle that it can actually produce wine at all. So how are the barely ripe grapes that are produced there turned into the world's most glorious sparkling wine?

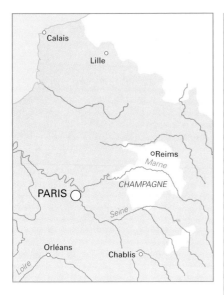

Champagne

By themselves, the grapes that go into Champagne (Chardonnay, Pinot Noir and Pinot Meunier) make thin, acidic wines. What transforms them is the addition of sugar and yeast, which causes a secondary fermentation in the bottle, producing the famous bubbles. The residue left over from this process (the lees) gives Champagne its honeyed, biscuity flavor.

The longer the wine stays locked away in the cool damp cellars of Champagne, the richer the flavor becomes. Cheap, non-vintage Champagne spends about a year to eighteen months on its lees. An expensive, vintage Champagne spends several years. And the best Champagnes of all are only disgorged (have their sediment removed) just

before they are released onto the market. This enables them to maintain a marvellously fresh taste despite their considerable age.

Each Champagne "house" (producer) produces several different styles of Champagne (*see also* pages 22–3). The bulk of its sales come from its non-vintage blend, which is made in a similar style from one year to the next. Every so often, when the harvest is sufficiently good, it will release a vintage Champagne (for instance in 1990). Most houses also release a *blanc de blancs* (Chardonnay only), rosé and a *demi-sec* (medium-dry) Champagne; some houses produce a top quality *prestige cuvée* such as Dom Pérignon.

Although the shelves are dominated by the big, famous names such as Lanson, Mumm and Moët et Chandon, you can get equally good value from lesser-known brands, and from so-called "growers' Champagnes." These are made by small producers who own their own vineyards (and may also grow grapes for the big houses). The best vineyards are designated Grand Cru, a term that doesn't carry quite the same weight as it does in Burgundy (*see* pages 94–5), but is a reasonable indication of quality.

Above: In the cellars of Champagne Taittinger in Reims bottles are still turned by hand.

Reading Champagne labels

At the top is a label from a famous Champagne house – a top-quality vintage Champagne. By contrast the label below is from a "grower" who produces his own wines – less well-known but by no means inferior.

① EXTRA CUVÉE DE RÉSERVE

② CHAMPAGNE

Pol Roger

A EPERNAY ③ ④ FRANCE

⑤ e 750 ml ⑥ Elaboré par Pol Roger, Epernay, France. 12%/vol. ⑦

N.M. 276-001

⑧ BRUT 1990

PRODUCE OF FRANCE

⑨

① **Extra Cuvée de Réserve** name of blend
② **Champagne** appellation
③ **Pol Roger** producer (classic large Champagne house)
④ **A Epernay, France** at Epernay
⑤ **750ml** size of bottle
⑥ **Elaboré par Pol Roger, Epernay, France** made by Pol Roger, etc
⑦ **12% vol** alcoholic strength
⑧ **Brut 1990** the style of wine, *brut* (bone dry) from 1990 (an excellent vintage)
⑨ **Produce of France**

① CHAMPAGNE
APPELLATION D'ORIGINE CONTROLEE ②
③ FLEURON 1990
④ 1er CRU
⑦ CÉPAGE NOBLE CHARDONNAY
⑧ BLANC DE BLANCS
⑤ *Pierre Gimonnet & Fils*
⑨ BRUT
VIGNOBLES: SUR LES TERROIRS DE CUIS, CRAMANT ET CHOUILLY
⑩ 12%alc./vol. ⑪ 750 ml
⑥ RM-22101-01
ELABORE PAR S.A. PIERRE GIMONNET & FILS à 51530 CUIS - FRANCE
⑫

① **Champagne**
② **appellation d'origine contrôlée** appellation Champagne
③ **Fleuron 1990** the name given to this particular blend (cuvée) and the vintage (very good year)
④ **1er cru** classification of the vineyards (good quality)
⑤ **Pierre Gimonnet et Fils** name of the producer (a well-regarded grower specialising in *blanc de blancs*)
⑥ **Vignobles: sur les terroirs de Cuis, Cramant et Chouilly** the location of the vineyards. These three villages are particularly good for Chardonnay
⑦ **Cépage noble Chardonnay** noble grape variety Chardonnay
⑧ **Blanc de blancs** style of Champagne made entirely from Chardonnay
⑨ **Brut** bone dry
⑩ **12% alc/vol** alcoholic strength
⑪ **750ml** bottle size
⑫ **Elaboré par SA Pierre Gimonnet & Fils à 51530 Cuis, France** the name and address of the producer

Other French sparkling wines

Even though other French sparkling wines are made by a similar method to Champagne, they're not allowed, by the European Union, to say so. So, most use the name *crémant* (meaning "sparkling") instead. The wines from the regions that are closest to Champagne, Crémant d'Alsace and Crémant de Bourgogne, are, as you might expect, the most similar in character. Crémant de Bourgogne is made, like Champagne, principally from Pinot Noir and Chardonnay; Crémant d'Alsace uses Pinot Blanc, Pinot Noir and Pinot Gris.

Elsewhere in France the term *crémant* tends to be an indication that the producer is using a significant proportion of Chardonnay. As a result, you can expect a wine that is quite creamy in character, similar in style to a *blanc de blancs* Champagne.

The Loire has a tradition of making sparkling wines from the Chenin Blanc grape. The best examples are Saumur Brut (which tends to be quite light, dry and yeasty) and the more honeyed Vouvray Mousseux (which can be dry or medium-dry).

Down in the Languedoc, the Limoux area produces the attractively soft, appley Blanquette de Limoux, which the locals claim to be the oldest sparkling wine in France, predating Champagne. Over in the Rhône, they make a deliciously light, grapey sparkling wine called Clairette de Die – not unlike Italian Asti. While none of these wines has the cachet or class of Champagne at its best, they can offer exceptionally good value.

Champagne-speak:

The trickiest things about Champagne are the terms that are used to indicate how dry or sweet it is. Most Champagnes you'll come across are *brut*, which means dry, but the less common *sec* (literally dry), in fact, means off-dry. *Demi-sec* means medium-dry, but for most tastes it's sweet enough to drink with dessert. *Doux* and *moelleux* are sweeter still. A more recent innovation is *rich*, a Champagne that has a touch of sweetness, but is basically a full-bodied style designed to go with rich foods, such as *foie gras*. It's also surprisingly successful with spicy cuisines.

Germany

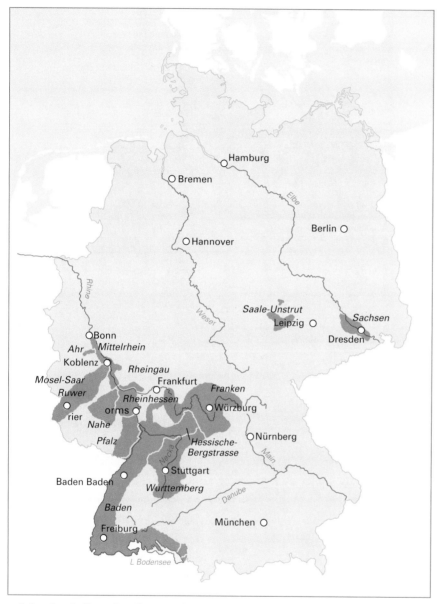

Riesling

Basically, Germany is a one-grape country. The Riesling grape towers over everything else. It is remarkable for its pure fruit flavors, which range from crisp apple to ripe peach and nectarine. But the most miraculous thing is how the flavors change and develop from the crisp tartness of a young wine to the complex lime, honey and kerosene flavors of a more mature one (*see* pages 64–5 and 86–7).

Mosel Rieslings (*see* below) can be as low as seven percent in alcohol and rarely rise above 10 percent.

Wine regions

Most of Germany's vineyards are clustered in the southwest of the country, around its major rivers, the Mosel and the Rhine. The most distinctive and highly prized area is the northerly Mosel-Saar-Ruwer, which produces the finest, raciest Rieslings on the planet (the Saar's being the steeliest of all). Other areas are less easy to pigeonhole. It used to be the case that the Pfalz (formerly Rheinpfalz) and Rheinhessen were the workhorse regions, churning out vast quantities of basic, cheap wines. However, Rheinhessen has its good producers and, these days, the Pfalz is regarded as one of the most dynamic wine-producing areas in Germany. Producers such as Burklin-Wolf and Müller-Catoir are doing much to restore Germany's reputation as a fine wine producer. The Rheingau and the Nahe, which both produce a riper, fruitier style of Riesling than

It's hard to believe that Germany's wines were once regarded as among the finest in Europe. Today they are, without doubt, the most underrated. Germany's once great reputation has been destroyed by a stream of bland, sugary whites such as Liebfraumilch – so much so that consumers have only to see a distinctive flute-like bottle to dismiss it immmediately.

This is a tragedy because Germany still offers some of most sensational white wines of any country in the world. Deliciously light, low in alcohol and infinitely refreshing, their delicate sweetness is balanced by a fine acidity making them capable of lasting – and improving – for years. They should have a place in everyone's wine collection.

the Mosel, are also well regarded. Drier whites come from the more southerly region of Baden, and from Franken to the east.

German wine terms

German wines are divided into four categories:

Tafelwein – literally table wine. Only from Germany if it says Deutscher Tafelwein. Generally very basic, though some producers, disenchanted with the official system chose to market their best wines as a Tafelwein in much the same way as do the Italians with vini da tavola (*see* pages 108–111).

Deutscher Landwein – a step up from Tafelwein – a wine that has some regional identity.

QbA (Qualitätswein bestimmter Anbaugebiete) – in theory better than Tafelwein or Landwein. In practice it can be used for Liebfraumilch.

QmP (Qualitätswein mit Prädikat) – the main indication of quality, based on how ripe the grapes that are used to make the wine were when picked. There are six categories, three of which relate to dry or off-dry wines (*see* below), and three to dessert wines (*see* over).

Some producers such as those from the Rheingau who don't feel the official classification offers the consumer enough of a guarantee of quality, have banded together to set up their own system, based on more rigorous standards. Look for wines labeled Charta or VDP.

Common areas of confusion

It's easy to confuse some of Germany's least-distinguished wines with its best. The villages of Nierstein, Piesport and Bernkastel, for example, give their names to three highly commercial wines: Niersteiner Gutes Domtal, Piesporter Michelsberg and Bereich Bernkastel. But each village also contains vineyards that produce fine wines such as Niersteiner Pettenthal, Piesporter Goldtröpfchen and Bernkasteler Doctor. Price is generally a reliable indication of quality – these top-quality vineyard wines don't come cheap. And the word *Bereich,* which merely means district, should warn you that you're not getting anything special.

Sweetness

The most important thing you need to know when you're buying a German

Above: Spätburgunder vines at Assmanshausen make some of Germany's finest reds.

wine is how sweet – or dry – it is. Cheaper wines are simply labeled *Trocken* (dry) or *Halbtrocken* (medium-dry). Better quality (QmP) wines are labelled *Kabinett*, *Spätlese* or *Auslese*. *Kabinett* wines are generally fresh, crisp and dry, while *Spätlese* (literally "late-picked") wines are richer and more honeyed, verging in some cases on sweet. (There is some variation, however, between different regions. Wines from warmer areas in Germany, such as the Rheingau or Pfalz, tend to be fruitier and less austere than those from the Mosel.)

Auslese is the tricky one. If it is inexpensive, it is generally medium-dry, even sweet. But *Auslesen* from first-rate producers will be a lot more opulent and honeyed – sweet, compared to, for instance, a Chablis, but still sufficiently dry to partner savory dishes (particularly duck, goose and fine oriental cuisine). They also become noticeably less sweet with age.

Sweet wines

Apart from *Auslese*, Germany has three grades of sweet wines: *Beerenauslese* and *Trockenbeerenauslese* (TBA), which are made from selected grapes that have been allowed to reach intense levels of ripeness and *Eiswein* which, as its name suggests, is made from frozen grapes (which are

Below: Full-bodied, yet silky, Rieslings come from these superb south-facing vineyards at Rüdesheim on the Rhine.

often not harvested until after Christmas). The right conditions don't always exist to produce TBAs and *Eisweins*, which makes them highly prized and consequently extremely expensive. All three styles are intensely sweet but are kept in perfect balance by piercing levels of acidity.

Drier whites

It is a myth that all German whites are made in an aromatic or off-dry style. In fact, winemakers are increasingly experimenting with drier styles – and getting mixed results. Often German wines need a touch of sweetness to offset their naturally high levels of acidity. The most distinctive wines are being made in warmer areas such as Baden and the Pfalz, from grapes other than Riesling – particularly Scheurebe, Weissburgunder (Pinot Blanc) and Ruländer or Grauerburgunder (alternative names for Pinot Gris). They're stylish and tend to be expensive. Many producers of cheaper, dry whites, such as Rivaner, are now packaging them in non-traditional Burgundy- or Bordeaux-shaped bottles, although this doesn't disguise the basic dullness of the contents.

Red wines

Surprisingly, 20 percent of the wines Germany produces are red, though only a small proportion is exported. They range from light and Beaujolais-like, to rich and plummy but without a lot of tannin. The most commonly planted grapes are Dornfelder, Lemberger (Austria's Blaufränkisch), Portugieser and Spätburgunder (Pinot Noir), which is generally made in a spicier, more robust style than is

Reading German labels

German wine labels are generally highly detailed and crammed with intimidating long words. Some forward-looking producers are labeling their bottles in a clearer, more consumer-friendly way, but, nevertheless, it is worth looking at a more standard label.

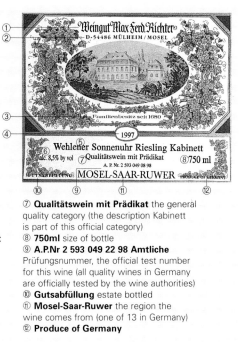

① **Weingut Max Ferd. Richter** Max Ferd. Richter wine estate (top Mosel estate)
② **D-54486 Mülheim/Mosel** Address
③ **Familienbesitz seit 1680** family-owned since 1680
④ **1997** vintage
⑤ **Wehlener Sonnenuhr Riesling Kabinett** Wehlener Sonnenuhr – a specific vineyard (Einzellage) in the Mülheim district of the Mosel; **Riesling Kabinett** the grape variety and its level of ripeness (ie quite light and crisp)
⑥ **alc. 8.5% vol** alcoholic strength (considerably lower in Germany than in most other wine-producing countries)

⑦ **Qualitätswein mit Prädikat** the general quality category (the description Kabinett is part of this official category)
⑧ **750ml** size of bottle
⑨ **A.P.Nr 2 593 049 22 98 Amtliche** Prüfungsnummer, the official test number for this wine (all quality wines in Germany are officially tested by the wine authorities)
⑩ **Gutsabfüllung** estate bottled
⑪ **Mosel-Saar-Ruwer** the region the wine comes from (one of 13 in Germany)
⑫ **Produce of Germany**

typical in Burgundy. Most of the best producers, such as Lingenfelder, come from the Pfalz.

Sekt

Sekt is Germany's sparkling wine – highly popular in the country itself but, to be honest, not terribly serious

Above: These Mosel vineyards are so steep that the vines are trained vertically.

competition for sparkling wines elsewhere. If you want to sample it go for "Deutscher Sekt," which will be made from German-grown grapes rather than just "Sekt," which may contain imported wine.

Why are top German wines so expensive?

Given the cheapness of the vast majority of German wines, it might seem odd that its top wines are so expensive. But winemaking in Germany is a risky enterprise. Not only do producers have to contend with the cool climate of this northerly growing region (which is on the same parallel as Labrador – 50°), but many of their vineyards are on precipitous slopes that can only be harvested by hand. And in order to get the intensity of flavor they are looking for, they have to severely restrict the number of bunches each vine produces.

Italy

Considering the Italians have been making and drinking wine for some 3,000 years, it seems strange that their wines are generally much less well-known than those of the French. Partly, of course, it's their own fault. Many of the popular Italian wines such as Chianti and Soave have been abysmally poor in quality, and the good ones overpriced. But another barrier is that it's just tremendously difficult to get a grip on the innumerable different wines and grape varieties the country produces.

Yet in a world where wines are becoming more and more similar, Italy has a great deal to offer. Its wines are amazingly varied, with quirky individual flavors that you don't find anywhere else. The one common thread is that they tend to have a higher than usual level of acidity that makes them go wonderfully well with food. Which, of course, is exactly how the Italians drink them.

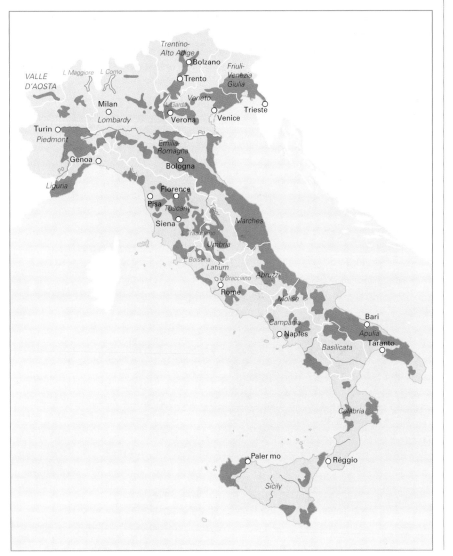

What Italy does well

Italy is still far more a red-wine country than a white, able to boast some fine, long-lived (and expensive) red wines, as well some charmingly light and simple ones. The thing that strikes you about them is how supple they are – not a bold block of flavor like many New World wines, but (at their best at least) light, smooth and elegant. Whites on the whole are crisp, fresh and dry – without the obvious fruitiness of, for example, a Chardonnay or a Sauvignon but, again, very flexible with food (*see* page 35).

Italian grapes

Try and memorize Italian grapes and you'll end up with a headache. For the most part they bear absolutely no relation to the name of the wine. The four that are worth remembering are: Pinot Grigio, which now tends to provide reasonably reliable drinking; Sangiovese and Barbera, with their distinctive bitter-sweet flavors; and big, beefy Nebbiolo, the grape that is used to make Barolo. These are the grapes many winemakers in the New World are taking an interest in to add greater variety to their winemaking.

Italy's main wine regions
Piedmont

Piedmont has built its reputation on two wines – Barolo and Barbaresco – that most people don't get to drink a lot of, partly because they're expensive, partly because they take years to mature. Both are made from the tannic Nebbiolo grape and traditionally make massive, dense, full-bodied wines.

More affordable are Barbera, which makes distinctive, bitter-sweet reds, and Dolcetto, which is softer, warmer and more brambly, but both these varieties can make serious wines too.

Curiously, the other main wine to come from the region – light, sweet sparkling Asti – couldn't be more different. And there are some attractive dry whites. Gavi is the most fashionable, although wine labeled Cortese (same grape as used for Gavi) provides better value for the money.

The Veneto and the northeast

This is predominantly white-wine territory, though it also produces some attractive light reds. The Veneto – the area round Venice – is responsible for many of the cheapest (and dullest) wines in the country – but, as elsewhere in Italy, quality has improved enormously. Its two most famous exports are Soave and Valpolicella.

Some of Italy's classiest (and most expensive) whites come from Friuli Venezia-Giulia, to the east and the Alto Adige, to the north, which tend to market their wines by grape variety. You'll find some of the best Chardonnay and Sauvignon from this area, alongside top-quality Pinot Grigio and Pinot Bianco. To the west, around Lake Garda, there are two other good whites to look for – smooth, creamy Lugana and Bianco di Custoza, both similar in style to Soave.

Central Italy

As far as the world at large is concerned, Italy is Tuscany. And Italian wine is Chianti, even if we no longer drink it from raffia-covered

Above: Chianti Rufina vineyards, Tuscany, produce one of the best-quality Chiantis.

Above: Nebbiolo vines close to Gattinara in Piedmont produce one of Italy's finest reds.

bottles. It varies hugely in style from simple, light, fruity reds, to very serious long-lived wines – in a very similar way to Bordeaux, in fact. The area in which Chianti is produced is divided into seven zones, the most important of which are Chianti Classico and Chianti Rufina. Wines that are labeled *riserva* have to have been aged in oak for two years.

Tuscany's top wine, however, is not Chianti but Brunello di Montalcino – also made like Chianti from the Sangiovese grape – but it has a much fuller-bodied style and is designed for long ageing. It is rivaled by a band of equally expensive wines, dubbed the Super-Tuscans, whose producers ignore the traditional regulations, use international grape varieties, such as Cabernet Sauvignon and Merlot, and age them in new oak barrels – rather than the traditional oak casks.

Other less-pricey reds from central Italy, that offer a good alternative to Chianti, are Rosso di Montalcino, and, two wines from the east coast, Rosso Conero and Montepulciano d'Abruzzo (both made from the Montepulciano grape). This is not to be confused with Vino Nobile di Montepulciano, another Brunello-style red named after the Tuscan town where it's made.

Whites definitely play second fiddle to reds in Tuscany; do look for the charming Vernaccia di San Gimignano, made in the hillside town just outside Florence. For alternatives you have to travel to Umbria (which produces the much improved Orvieto) or Rome for its fresh, fruity Frascati. Verdicchio, which comes from the Marches, is also a good seafood white.

Southern Italy and the islands

The south of Italy is the area that everyone is really getting excited about. Due to its reliable climate, it has always been regarded – like the Languedoc in France – as a cheap source of bulk wine. Even now, only two percent of the wine Puglia produces is bottled, but that all seems about to change.

What these warmer areas already have to offer is a highly individual style of warm, sweet, raisiny red wine, based on local grapes such as Aglianico, Negroamaro, Nero d'Avola and

Buying Italian wine

The main problem with Italian wine is the huge variations in quality. Take Valpolicella. The vast majority of basic wines are light, fruity and gluggable. But there are producers such as Allegrini, Masi and Tedeschi who produce wines that are much more powerfully flavored. (To complicate the picture there are also a couple of quirky styles of Valpolicella – Amarone and the sweet Recioto della Valpolicella – which are almost port-like in their intensity.) How to separate the sheep from the goats? Avoid any wine under 12 degrees. Avoid cut-price bargains. And ideally buy from an Italian specialist or on a recommendation from a wine guide.

Reading Italian labels

These two labels illustrate the inadequacies of Italian wine classification. The top one is a DOCG wine, technically, the highest ranking, but not always the guarantee of quality it might seem. The second is a seemingly lowly *vino da tavola* wine, but, in fact, is an illustrious, highly sought-after Cabernet-based Super-Tuscan wine. Both come from the well-known producer, Antinori, who has chosen to make wine both in and out of the official classification system – basically so that he can grow the grape varieties and produce the styles he wants.

① **Tenute** estate
② **Marchese Antinori** producer's name (very reliable company)
③ **Riserva** aged in oak barrels for two years
④ **Chianti Classico** the area of production, the higher quality, central part of the Chianti region
⑤ **Denominazione di origine controllata e garantita** offficially the top Italian wine category. But the producer's name is a greater reassurance
⑥ **1985** the vintage
⑦ **750ml** size of bottle
⑧ **Imbottigiato in San Casciano V.P. (382 FI) de Marchesi L. e P. Antinori S. p. A. Firenzi Italia** bottled in San Casciano by Antinori, which has its head-office in Florence
⑨ **12.5% vol.** alcoholic strength
⑩ **Italia** product of Italy

① **Vino da Tavola di Toscana** the classification, techically the lowest ranking (but the high price of this wine would have immediately indicated that this is misleading)
② **Non disperdere il vetro nell'ambiente** this is asking you to dispose of the bottle thoughtfully
③ **Solaia** the name of the wine (a famous Cabernet-based Super-Tuscan)
④ **Marchesi Antinori** the producer
⑤ **Firenzi** Florence, where Antinori is based
⑥ **1990** the vintage
⑦ **Imbottiglio in San Casciano V. P. da Marchesi Antinori S.r.l. Firenzi Italia** the producer's details, as above
⑧ **750ml** size of bottle
⑨ **13% vol** alcoholic strength
⑩ **Italia** product of Italy

Primitivo. Wines to look for if you like this style are Salice Salentino, Copertino and Squinzano from Puglia, Aglianico del Vulture, which comes from Basilicata, and Carignano from Sardinia.

But the big expansion is coming as a result of foreign investment and flying winemakers, who are pouring into Puglia and Sicily to make inexpensive, fruity wines in a more modern style. Despite using varieties such as Merlot and Chardonnay, they are blending them with local grapes to produce wines with more individual flavors. Expect to see many more of them.

Italian fizz

I use the word "fizz" deliberately because many Italian wines are only slightly fizzy or *frizzante*. Italians also have a taste for wines that are off-dry. Moscato d'Asti is the best of the wines that come from around Asti, but there's also Prosecco (produced in the Veneto region) and, of course, Lambrusco (from the Emilia-Romagna region) – not the dull, sugar-sweet confection that gets exported, but an exuberant, frothy, red sparkling wine that can be a delight.

Vin Santo

Probably the most fashionable Italian wine of the moment is not a red but a dessert wine, Vin Santo, served with *cantucci* biscuits to dip in it. Although it is produced throughout Italy, most comes from Tuscany and fetches the same extravagant prices as the Super-Tuscans. A less expensive alternative is the glorious apricot-scented Passito di Pantelleria, which comes from a tiny Italian-owned island (Pantelleria) just off the North African coast.

Above: Fresh modern wines are now made in Puglia at the historic heel of Italy.

Spain

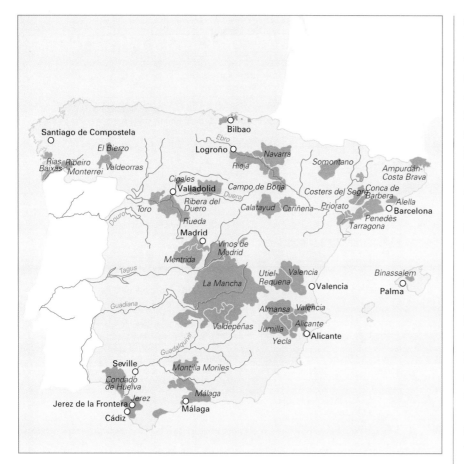

The most important Spanish grape, which gives such distinctive sweet strawberry-and-vanilla flavor to its oak-aged reds, is Tempranillo. But, just to complicate things, they call it by different names in different parts of Spain – Tinto Fino in Ribera del Duero and Cencibel in Valdepeñas. Also gaining wider recognition is Garnacha (Grenache), particularly from old vines that produce intensely concentrated fruit.

Other grape varieties you may find on labels are Monastrell (France's Mourvèdre) and Cariñena (Carignan), both of which make big, beefy reds. Viura is the variety used for white Rioja (also known as Macabeo) and Verdejo is the backbone of fresh, appley Rueda.

Spanish wine terms

The most useful things to master about Spanish reds are the terms that describe oak ageing. *Joven* is a young wine, generally unoaked and released within a year of the harvest.

Wines labeled *Crianza* and *Reserva* both have to have spent a year in oak barrels, but a *Crianza* is released after two years and a *Reserva* after three. That generally (but not invariably) makes *Reserva* wines taste softer and oakier than *Crianza* wines, which can be quite vibrant and fruity.

Gran Reserva wines, which are not released until they're five years old, must have spent two years in oak and have the capacity to last for a good deal longer.

I f I asked you to name six Spanish wines you'd probably get stuck after Rioja. For a country that has the most extensive vineyards in the world, Spain's wines are remarkably poorly known. The main reason is that, with one or two exceptions, Spain has concentrated on producing quantity rather than quality. But also many people don't get the same opportunity to try Spanish wine, as they do Italian wine, because there aren't that many Spanish restaurants outside Spain.

Spain's main strength is a reliably hot climate, producing red wines able to stand up to long oak ageing. In the past that style has been overwhelmingly favored by local winemakers. But times are changing here, as everywhere else in the wine world, and these days Spain is producing much bolder, fruitier reds from international grape varieties such as Cabernet and Merlot, as well as indigenous varieties such as Tempranillo.

Despite the arrival of foreign winemakers, Spain has managed to preserve its identity. Although it produces a huge amount of basic red and white from the vast vineyards of Valencia and La Mancha, it has a host of small and highly individual wine regions with distinctive flavors to offer. And in most cases – particularly Cava and sherry (*see* over) – they're still an extraordinarily good value.

Rioja and other oak-aged reds

Rioja's role as Spain's foremost red wine is recognized by the fact it comes into a quality category of its own – DOC (*denominacion de origen calificada*), not yet awarded to any other Spanish region. Famous for its very traditional, oak-aged wines, the region is changing rapidly, with the biggest differences no longer being between the three sub-sections of the region (Rioja Alavesa, Alta and Baja), but between producers who use new oak and modern grape varieties, and those who stick to the original oak casks. Among the former are Artadi, Martinez Bujanda, Marques de Griñon and Cosme Palacio; other producers, such as Campo Viejo, straddle both styles.

The wines of the Navarra region are very similar to those of Rioja, although producers there are even more likely to use international grape varieties.

Less well-known, except by wine connoisseurs who accumulate its flagship wine, Vega Sicilia, is Ribera del Duero – considered by many to be the top wine-producing region in Spain. Although its wines are made from the same grape variety as Rioja – Tempranillo (here called Tinto Fino) – they tend to be more full-bodied and less fruity than Rioja, with a distinctive savory, almost bacon-like character.

Even more in demand are the intensely flavored wines of Priorato, a tiny wine-producing area in the south of Spain that has achieved cult status (and correspondingly high prices). It has the distinction of requiring its wines to have a minimum alcohol

Above: Vineyards around the village of Paganos, Rioja Alavesa.

Reading Spanish labels

The key to understanding Spanish labels is to look for certain key words that indicate how much or little time the wine has spent in oak barrels. The wine on the right is a young wine, the wine below is a more mature, oaky *Reserva*.

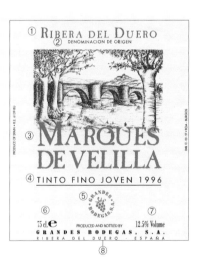

① **Ribera del Duero** area the wine comes from
② **Denominacion de origen** classification
③ **Marquès de Velilla** name of the wine
④ **Tinto Fino Joven 1996** Tinto Fino - the grape variety (Tempranillo); **Joven** young wine, released within a year of the harvest (generally unoaked); **1996** vintage
⑤ **Grandes Bodegas S.A.** the producer
⑥ **75cl** – size of bottle
⑦ **12.5% volume** alcoholic strength
⑧ **Produced and bottled by Grandes Bodegas, S.A. Ribera del Duero, España** name and address of company

① **Rioja** area the wine comes from
② **Denominacion de origen calificada** the classification (Rioja is as yet the only region to use this term, the others just use 'denominacion de origen')
③ **Bottled by Bodegas Campo Viejo. S.A.** name of the producer (a well-established company)
④ **Logroño, Rioja Alta, España** the producer's address
⑤ **750ml** – size of bottle
⑥ **Alc.12.5 by vol.** alcoholic strength
⑦ **Reserva 1991** This was harvested in 1991 and will have spent at least a year in oak barrels and up to two in the bottle before release

content of 13.5 percent. At the other end of the price spectrum, making traditional, but often very good-value reds, are the regions of Jumilla, Toro, Valdepeñas and Yecla.

New-wave reds

It seems highly appropriate that many of the country's most innovative winemaking areas are within striking distance of Barcelona, Spain's hippest city. The Catalan regions of Costers del Segre, Conca de Barbera, Penedès and Tarragona have all been in the vanguard of Spain's wine revolution, led by producers such as Raimat,

León and Torres. The result of this is a much softer, more accessible style of red wine made from international varieties such as Cabernet, Merlot and Syrah.

Other regions to watch for include Calatayud to the south of Rioja, Somontano, which lies in the foothills of the Pyrenees, Utiel Requena in Valencia and Bierzo up in the northwest.

New-wave whites

Spain's whites – never its strong point – have seen the biggest leap in quality. Even basic Spanish whites are

Above: Raïmat's state-of-the-art winery near Laida in Catalonia shows that modern wineries don't have to be purely functional, but present an opportunity for some stunning architecture.

decent now, but for something with a bit more character try some of the crisp, citrussy whites now being produced in Rueda, Rioja and (in tiny quantities) in Alella. Spain's most fashionable white, however, is an elegant, aromatic wine called Albariño, which is produced in the Rías Baixas region, on the northwest coast, near the Portuguese border.

Inevitably Chardonnay, too, plays a part. Spanish producers in areas such as Navarra, Somontano and Penedès tend to favor a rich, oaky style as befits their hot climate.

Cava

Cava, which is produced mainly in Penedès, in the northeast of Spain, has to get the prize for the most drinkable, inexpensive sparkling wine in the world. Crisp, dry and yeasty, it's a more than acceptable cut-price substitute for cheap Champagne. Although it's mainly made from local Spanish grapes, quality has been improved by blending in Chardonnay.

Vintage versions vary. They can be good, but you may not consider them worth the extra money if you prefer a fresher style of fizz (though you can scarcely argue that prices are greedy). There are attractive rosé versions too.

Sweet wines

Spain isn't a big producer of sweet wines but has one outstanding bargain you should be aware of – Moscatel de Valencia, a deliciously grapey dessert wine, that you could drink as easily before a meal as at the end of it. Better quality versions often have a pronounced orange-peel flavor.

Rosé

In many areas of Spain they traditionally drink rosé (*rosado*) rather than white. It tends to be more robust than many rosés – the most common grape variety being Garnacha, which produces vivid strawberry-flavored wines. The best examples tend to come from Navarra.

Sherry

Real sherry (and Spanish producers have had to spend a lot of time dealing with competition from inferior wines that passed themselves off as sherry) comes from a strictly limited area of southern Spain called Jerez. Far superior in quality to its imitators, it offers a fabulous range of flavors that totally belie its stuffy image.

There are two main types of sherry – fino and oloroso. Fino is protected during the three-year ageing process by a thick layer of yeast called *flor*, which preserves its pale color and gives it a very refreshing, clean, yeasty flavor that can almost taste like green olives. Manzanilla, which comes from the coastal town of Sanlúcar de Barrameda, is a very pungent fino, with a pronounced salty tang.

Amontillado is fino sherry that has been left to age in oak for several years, during which time it acquires a rich nutty, toffee flavor. A variation on that is Palo Cortado, which is slightly darker and richer.

Olorosos go through a different production process, being fortified after the wine has fermented so that the *flor* doesn't develop. They can be dry (*seco*) or sweet (*dulce*), but tend to be darker in color than an amontillado, with rich fruitcake flavors. The sweetest sherry of all is Pedro Ximénez, an intensely dark, treacly sherry, so thick you can (and should) pour it over ice-cream.

When you think of the amount of work that goes into producing sherry, and the costs of keeping it for years, it is actually astonishingly cheap. The most expensive bottles, which may contain sherries that have been aged for decades, cost about the same as a non-vintage Champagne.

Montilla is Spain's other main fortified wine, made in similar styles to sherry. It can also be a good value but rarely achieves similar levels of quality.

Storage and serving

Contrary to what many people think, sherry is not designed to be poured into a decanter and left in a cupboard. Fino sherry should be treated like white wine, chilled before serving and then drunk up within a couple of days of opening. (For this reason it makes sense to buy it in half-bottles.) Amontillado and oloroso sherries can be kept longer once opened, but are still best drunk within a month. Both styles of sherry should ideally be served in a traditional Spanish-style *copita* glass with a tapered rim.

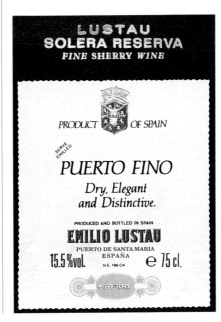

Portugal

The last decade has seen a revolution in Portuguese winemaking. Although you can, and still do, come across the old-fashioned, heavily oaked reds that were typical of the country, Portugal has suddenly become one of the most exciting and innovative wine producers in Europe – and, better still, one that offers exceptional value for the money.

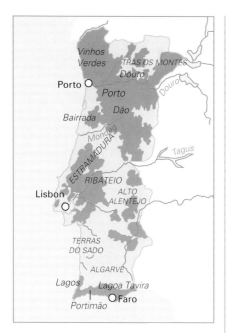

Grape varieties

Portugal's great strength is that it has stuck to what it does well – making full, fruity reds. Unlike other countries, it didn't rush to rip up old vines and plant Cabernet and Merlot. It has a mass of grape varieties of its own – so many that it's impossible to keep track of them (not least because the names change from one region to another).

One variety that is worth remembering, because it produces particularly attractive, soft, supple wines, is Periquita. But the most influential are the five grape varieties that are used to make port: Touriga Nacional, Tinta Barroca, Tinta Cão,

Touriga Francesca and Tinta Roriz (the same grape as Spain's Tempranillo). In fact, if you think of Portuguese reds as a slightly less-alcoholic, less-sweet version of port, with the same kind of warm, rich, spicy, brambly fruit, you get a very good idea of what the wines are like.

Portuguese whites tend to be less distinguished. The best-known is Vinho Verde, a light, dry, slightly spritzy white; the kind of wine that tastes much better on the spot than it does when you find it in your local supermarket. But progressive winemakers are beginning to produce more characterful examples with local grape varieties,

that offer a real alternative to internationally grown grapes such as Chardonnay and Sauvignon.

Surprisingly (considering one of the best-known wines in the world during the '60s and '70s was the distinctively shaped bottle of Mateus Rosé), Portugal doesn't make much rosé. The medium-dry style of Mateus has fallen from favor, but Portugal has more than enough red-wine grapes to start producing rosé in quantity, should it ever come back into fashion.

Regions

In general, the most serious red wines are made in the north of the country – chiefly in the port-producing region of the Douro, which has access to the country's best grapes. To the south of here are two adjoining regions, Dão and Bairrada. Dão, the larger and

Above: Grape picking in the Quinta do Vesuvio, high above the Douro River.

better-known of the two, is renowned for its lengthily aged, oaky reds, though fruitier, more modern styles are now emerging. Bairrada used to produce rather tough tannic reds, from the local Baga grape, but, there again, the wines are becoming a lot more supple and fruity. Two newer and lesser-known regions to watch are Trás-os-Montes to the north of the Douro, and Beiras to the south of Dão.

Most of the country's cheaper, commercial wines come from two regions north of Lisbon – the Estremadura and the Ribatejo, which mainly produce light, uncomplicated, fruity reds. Ribatejo grapes are also traditionally used to make *garrafeira* wines (reserve-type wines that receive at least two years of oak ageing and another year in the bottle before being released). The other up-and-coming area around Lisbon is Setúbal, to the southeast, formerly known for a dark, treacly style of fortified wine. (Some particularly exciting new reds come from the district of Palmela nearby.)

The region that dominates the south of the country is the Alentejo – potentially the best wine-producing area outside the Douro. Look out particularly for wines from the northeast of the region from the DOCs* of Borba and Portalegre.

* Wines are classified as DOC (Denominação de Origem Controlada) and IPR (Indicação de Proviniência Regulamentada), which are effectively DOCs on probation. Wines that fall outside these rules are categorized as Vinhos Regional (a bit like a French vin de pays). They include many of the newer, more dynamic wine-producing areas such as the Alentejo.

Port

Like the majority of sherries, port is a fortified wine – one to which brandy has been added to boost its strength and preserve its sweetness. Although there are different types of port you'll probably find you prefer one of the two most characteristic styles – the warm, rich, brambly flavor of a Late-bottled Vintage port or the nuttier, more toffee-like taste of a 10-year-old tawny.

Ruby

Ruby port is the lightest and fruitiest port. It comes from grapes that have been blended and aged for two to three years in oak casks or stainless steel. Better-quality ruby ports go under a confusing variety of names, such as Special Reserve, Vintage Character and Late Bottled Vintage or LBV (port from a single vintage that is bottled four to six years after the harvest). Sweet, warming and spicy, it's a considerably more complex wine than either Vintage Character or Special Reserve Port. Most bottles can be drunk immediately without being decanted, except those described as Traditional or Bottle Matured, which accumulate a deposit like vintage port.

Tawny

The least expensive tawny ports are simply a blend of ruby and white port and have nothing like the delicious, nutty character of older tawny ports, that get their color and flavor from being aged in oak casks. The most common types are 10- and 20-year-old tawnies (10 and 20 being the average age of the wines in the blend). Less common – and far more expensive – are 30- and 40-year-old tawnies. Some Portuguese-owned producers (called "shippers" in the port trade) also release a *Colheita*, a tawny port that has been aged for at least seven years.

Vintage

Although there's a lot of talk about vintage port, it only accounts for less than one percent of port sales. The big difference from other ports is that it is bottled after only two years in wood, but must then be kept for at least another ten and preferably 15–20 years before drinking. During this time it accumulates a heavy sediment which is why it needs to be decanted (*see* pages 47). In style it is similar to an LBV, but much richer and mellower, with a sensuously soft, velvety texture.

Not every year's harvest is considered high enough quality to declare as a vintage. In other years, many port houses release what they call a Single Quinta Vintage, a high-quality port from one of their best estates.

Reading port labels

Port labels can be confusing because of the different use of the word "vintage." Genuine vintage ports just say "Vintage Port" on the label – not "Late Bottled Vintage" or "Vintage Character".

FERREIRA
1977
VINTAGE PORT

BOTTLED BY
A. A. FERREIRA, S. A. PORTO
PRODUCED AND BOTTLED IN PORTUGAL
20% Vol.   PRODUCE OF PORTUGAL   75 cl.

Central and Eastern Europe

Wines from Central and Eastern Europe are as different as the countries they come from, so it's easiest to think of them in two distinct groups: the wines that come from Austria and Switzerland, which are high quality, but expensive; and those from the former Eastern Bloc countries, which, by contrast, offer some of the most inexpensive drinking in the world. This is one of the areas of Europe where flying winemakers have been most active, so many of the wines consciously mimic New World styles.

Central Europe

Austria

Austria's wines are similar to those of Germany, but they benefit from a warmer climate. Austria certainly rivals Germany as one of the great sources of dessert wines, most of which are produced around the Neusiedler See, a huge lake on the Hungarian border. Austria's whites are mainly aromatic, mostly produced from the local Grüner Veltliner grape. Younger, inexpensive versions are crisp, fresh and appley, but top-quality ones, such as those produced in the Wachau region (which also produces fine Riesling), can age for many years.

Austria also produces some exotically flavored reds from local grapes such as Blaufränkisch, Blauer Portugieser, Zweigelt and St-Laurent. The best combine an incredible intensity of fruit with an appealing suppleness. Unfortunately most are consumed within Austria itself.

Switzerland

Most Swiss wines tend to come from the French-speaking part of the country. The majority are crisp, dry whites, made mainly from Chasselas (or Fendant as it is also known) and go well with the country's many cheese dishes.

Reds are principally Pinot Noir and Gamay (a common blend of the two is called Dôle), made in a soft, juicy Beaujolais style. There is also some Merlot, particularly in the Italian-speaking cantons to the south. Like Austrian wines, top Swiss wines tend to be expensive and rarely make it out of the country.

Eastern Europe

Bulgaria

Given the country's severe economic problems, Bulgaria's wineries have struggled to keep pace with the rest of the world. It is mainly a red-wine producer, and a very traditional one at that – most of its wines are still aged for several years in oak casks. It does, however, have great natural advantages, in the form of old vines and a warm climate that can ripen grapes reliably. It also has a vast acreage of Cabernet Sauvignon, which makes a convincing, inexpensive substitute for Bordeaux.

More youthful, exuberant reds are beginning to emerge in Bulgaria, made from Merlot and two local grapes, Gamza and Mavrud, and there is also some acceptable Chardonnay. This country's wines certainly have a lot of potential, but may take years to realize it.

Hungary

The most progressive and successful of the countries of the former Eastern Bloc, Hungary's great strength is its white wines, particularly cut-price versions of Europe's most popular grape varieties, Chardonnay and Sauvignon Blanc.

Hungary also has a whole raft of local, aromatic grape varieties, such as Furmint, Hárslevelü and Irsai Oliver (sometimes referred to as "poor man's Gewürztraminer"), which make fragrant, aromatic whites.

Its best-known red, the robust Bull's Blood, is unfortunately not what it once was, but lighter, more commercial reds are being made from grapes such as Merlot and Kékfrankos (the same grape as Austria's Blaufränkisch).

But, Hungary's great glory is the fabulous dessert wine Tokaji (Tokay), first made in the late 17th century and still regarded as one of the world's great dessert wines. Like Sauternes, it is made from grapes that are affected by "noble rot" or *aszu*, causing them to shrivel and produce an intensely sweet, syrupy paste. The sweetness of the wines is measured in *puttonyos*, the name of the containers in which the sweet concentrate is kept, six being the sweetest. The rarest and most prized kind of Tokaji is Essencia, and is believed to have aphrodisiac qualities. (Unfortunately it is not commercially available.)

Romania

Romania, like Bulgaria, suffers from severe lack of investment, but again has the potential to produce some fine reds. It is most renowned for a particularly rich, full-bodied style of Pinot Noir (*see* pages 67 and 72–3) but also produces some robust Cabernet and Merlot.

Other wine-producing countries of the region

Many of the other wine-producing countries of the region, including those of former Czechoslovakia, Yugoslavia and the USSR, are in a state of economic crisis, or political turbulence.

The countries that are currently exporting most are Slovakia and Slovenia but, unfortunately, we tend to see their least-interesting wines – light, sweet Riesling lookalikes, such as Slovenia's Lutomer Laski Rizling.

Moldova produces some creditable Chardonnay, while reds are best represented by the robust, brambly Vranac, which is grown in Montenegro and Macedonia.

Other countries that have the potential to develop their wine industries include Croatia, Yugoslavia Georgia, the Ukraine and Russia.

Above: These spectacular Swiss alpine vineyards produce delicious, but rare, wines.

North America

Although 47 of the United States – including Hawaii – grow grapes, when we talk about North American wine we are, in effect, talking about California. Not only in terms of volume (it accounts for well over 90 percent of the wine made in the States), but in terms of lifestyle too. Californians have a truly European-style food and wine culture. The majority of Americans (other than those on the East Coast) still rarely drink wine at all on average.

There's a similar imbalance within California itself. The image of Californian wines is of the world-class reds and whites that emerge from the expensive boutique wineries of the Napa Valley. But the reality is that almost 90 percent of Californian wine comes from the vast commercial vineyards to the south of San Francisco, which enables the US to vie with Argentina as the fourth biggest wine-producer in the world.

California's wine regions

California's vineyards are divided into AVAs – Approved Viticultural Areas. Some are based on whole counties, others on smaller subregions. Sonoma, for example, produces wine that is labeled Sonoma County, but it also encompasses Dry Creek, Alexander Valley, Chalk Hill, the Russian River Valley and part of Carneros, all of which have a distinct regional identity. As a result of the problems they have had with the devastating vine disease phylloxera, which has meant that whole vineyards have had to be ripped out and replanted, Californians have been among the first winemakers in the New World to recognize that particular areas suit certain grape varieties. For instance, in Carneros and the Russian River Valley you find mainly Pinot Noir and Chardonnay, in Alexander Valley and Dry Creek, Cabernet Sauvignon and Zinfandel, and in Atlas Peak, Sangiovese. It's the closest the New World gets to the classic wine regions of France.

Northern California

The area to the north of San Francisco produces California's finest wines. At the heart of it is a 26-mile-long strip of land called the Napa Valley, which rivals Burgundy's Côte d'Or as some of the most expensive vineyard land in the world. But even this tiny area experiences huge variations in temperature, from cool, fog-affected Carneros in the south, to much hotter regions, such as Howell Mountain, which is more suitable for growing full-bodied Cabernets and Zinfandels. This is home to California's First Growths – cult wines, such as Opus One, Dominus and Volcanic Hills, which fetch prices similar to the top wines from Bordeaux and Burgundy.

The other important area is the Sonoma Valley. It rivals Napa for quality, but produces generally more immediately drinkable – and affordable wines. This northern part of California also produces some of the best sparkling wines outside Champagne.

Central and southern California

The area south of San Francisco has two totally different climates. The Central Coast region, which runs down to Santa Barbara, is broadly

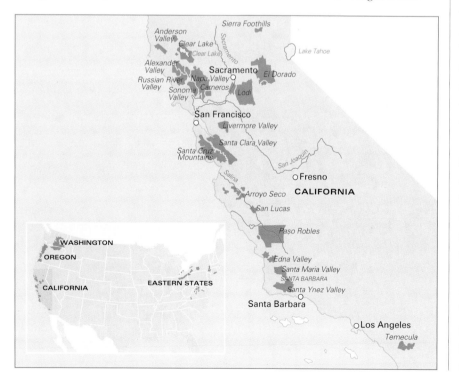

similar to the north, its temperature moderated by California's famous coastal fogs. It contains some fine winemaking areas, such as Santa Cruz and Monterey to the north, and the up-and-coming Edna and Santa Maria Valleys just outside Santa Barbara to the south, which are producing some exciting Pinot Noirs and Chardonnays. But the vast majority of California's wine comes from the stiflingly hot San Joaquin Valley to the east, part of the Central Valley region, which produces most of the state's inexpensive "jug" or table wines.

California crazes

In California, more than anywhere else, wines are subject to crazes. At one stage it was Fumé Blanc, a soft, oaky style of Sauvignon Blanc brilliantly marketed by Robert Mondavi. Then there was (and to some exent still is) Merlot mania. The new rising star is Viognier, a grape that makes an attractively aromatic style of dry white wine. But, Sangiovese could well be next in line.

Above: Vineyards in Oakville, Napa Valley, the heart of California wine production.

But this too has areas such as Lodi to the north that are beginning to forge a reputation for quality wines.

Grapes and wine styles

More than any other New-World country, the Californians model their wines on the French, seeking to emulate the top wines of Bordeaux and Burgundy. So California's wines tend to be concentrated on the same grape varieties – Chardonnay, Cabernet,

Merlot and Pinot Noir. Being California, however, they're all a little larger than life: huge, massively structured Cabernets that are designed to take on Bordeaux First Growths head-to-head; Merlot that is lusher and softer than anything St-Emilion has to offer; and big, buttery Chardonnays that make even Meursault taste mean. They may (to traditionalists at least) lack finesse, but they certainly don't lack flavor.

The same approach carries through to its less-expensive wines. Now that Australia is making Chardonnays in a lighter, fresher style, California is the last bastion of the big, oaky Chardonnay. The region's wines are often sweeter than elsewhere in the New World, catering to the palates of a wine-drinking public that still has a taste for off-dry wines. (Wines such as Colombard and White Zinfandel – Calfornia's equivalent of medium-dry German whites such as Liebfraumilch – are still very popular.)

At the opposite end of the spectrum are some highly individual wines, made by maverick winemakers such as Randall Grahm. His passion for the

Above: Demand for Californian wines has led to acres of new plantings.

grape varieties of the Rhône, such as Syrah, Grenache and Mourvèdre, led to the coining of the term "Rhône Rangers." Also increasingly popular (unsurprisingly in view of the number of former Italian immigrants in the state) are Italian-grape varieties, such as Barbera and Sangiovese. While the amount of wine made from these grapes is still comparatively modest, expect to see a lot more of them.

Zinfandel

Zinfandel is a grape that is virtually unique to California – although it is generally believed to be related to the Italian-grape variety Primitivo, which grows in southern Italy. Although the majority of grapes that are produced go to make medium-sweet "white" Zin, it's far more prized for the intense, brambly reds that are made from some of the state's oldest vines, dubbed by some of California's more offbeat producers as "power" or "killer" Zins. There are also smoother, less-blockbusting examples available from mainstream producers such as Gallo.

The Pacific Northwest

The most exciting wine-producing area outside California, the Pacific Northwest, consists of the states of Oregon, Washington and Idaho. They couldn't be more different. Oregon is like northern California, only more so – cool and damp – ideally suited to the production of the Burgundian-style Pinot Noirs that are its trademark. It also makes some fine Alsace-like aromatic wines, particularly Pinot Gris, Gewürztraminer and Riesling (dry and sweet). Washington, whose vineyards are situated on the other side of the towering Cascade Mountains, is much hotter and drier, better suited to making full-bodied reds – despite the fact that it has severely cold winters that tend to wipe out one in six harvests. Its Cabernets and Merlots already rival California's best, and Syrah could well follow suit. Idaho's climate is similar to Washington's, but even more subject to extremes of temperature.

New York

You might not think of New York City as having vines on its doorstep, but some of the best vineyards in the state are on Long Island – which manages to produce some fine reds (most of which unfortunately get snapped up by wine-loving New Yorkers).

Elsewhere in this large state, the main production areas are the Hudson Valley and the Finger Lakes, by Lake Ontario. Finger Lakes produces some fine Chardonnay, Riesling and Pinot Noir, as well as wines from less-familiar hybrids such as Seyval Blanc, Vidal, and Maréchal Foch, designed to withstand the rigors of the cool climate.

Other wine-producing states

Farther down the East Coast, Maryland and Virginia are other significant players. There is also a growing number of wine producers in Ohio, and in Missouri in the Midwest. Farther south, the most promising wine-producing areas are Texas and Arizona, which are producing predictably full-bodied reds.

Canada

You may think Canada is too cold to produce wine, but it does so in two areas where the temperatures are more moderate – British Columbia in the northwest, which produces the same type of wines as Oregon, and Ontario, which is very similar to New York's Finger Lakes. In both cases the cool climate dictates whites rather than reds (apart from Pinot Noir), and Chardonnay, in particular, can be excellent. But Canada's finest achievement is superb dessert wines – particularly ice wine that is on a par with Germany's best. Most of Canada's top-quality wines are labelled VQA, which means they conform to standards laid down by the Vintners' Quality Alliance.

Below: Long Island, NY is one of the East Coast's most dynamic wine regions.

South and Central America

The most exciting wine regions to open up in the last few years have been in Argentina and Chile. Though they might seem miles apart, their vineyards are, in fact, very close – Chile's wineries being clustered around its capital, Santiago, while most of Argentina's are based just over the Andes in Mendoza.

Because of the economic and political instability, both countries have been slow to get their wine industries off the ground compared with Australia and California, but they both have very real potential to make great wines.

The incredible success of the wine industry in the last few years, and subsequent demand for Chilean wine, has inevitably meant that it's not the bargain it once was. Almost all producers have given in to the temptation to make their own "Super-Chilean" red, some of which, such as Seña and Montes M, command very high prices indeed, and are designed to compete with the best wines from France, Italy and California.

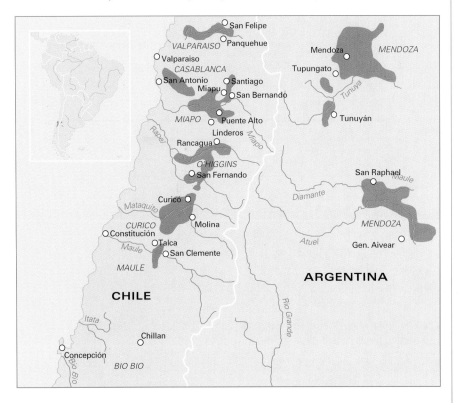

Argentina

If any country can satisfy the world's new-found appetite for red wine at a reasonable price it's Argentina. The world's fourth-largest wine producer, it's the great sleeping giant of the wine world, only just now beginning to produce the kind of wines the international market wants to drink.

Its big advantage over Chile is that it has a much wider range of grape varieties to work from, owing to successive waves of immigrants, particularly the Italians. In addition to Cabernet and Merlot, it has Syrah, Sangiovese, Barbera, Bonarda and Tempranillo. But it is Malbec, a grape that originates from southwest France and which is used in Bordeaux (*see* pages 92–3), that is creating the most excitement. Argentinian Malbec is smooth, rich, velvety and plummy, capable of lasting for years and will almost certainly result in very great wines.

Also promising is Syrah (which the Argentinians pronounce "sheerah") – more like the French version than

Chile

Chile has a near-perfect climate for growing grapes and the rare advantage of phylloxera-free vineyards. (Phylloxera is the louse that destroys vine roots, and devastated vineyards throughout France and much of Europe in the last century.) In fact, in an area also ideally suited to growing fruit, the problem is trying to prevent its vines growing too prolifically. Nevertheless, these conditions allow Chile to produce particularly soft, lush,

velvety reds. Merlot is the star grape variety, though Cabernet also achieves a level of ripeness and sweetness rarely managed anywhere else. Pinot Noir, Malbec and Syrah are also promising.

Chile's best white wines come from a cool, coastal region called Casablanca, which produces lively, lemony Sauvignons and crisp, citrussy Chardonnays (Chilean winemakers tend not to go in for the blockbuster style). There's also a limited amount of Gewürztraminer.

Australian Shiraz, but capable of producing the same big, peppery, blockbuster reds.

Argentinian whites are less interesting, though it makes some creditable Chardonnay. But, its most distinctive variety is Torrontes, a headily perfumed grape that tastes a bit like Gewürztraminer, and which makes delightful fresh, flowery young whites.

Argentina's great advantage is that there is so much land to explore and develop – from high-altitude Salta in the north, already producing crisp whites and intense minty Cabernets, to the cooler Rio Negro region down south, which may well prove suitable for fine Pinot Noir.

Brazil, Peru and Uruguay

Other countries in South America that make wine include Brazil, Peru, and Uruguay which has the most advanced wine industry. It also has a distinctive full-bodied red grape variety, Tannat, originally from Southwest France – but as yet makes nothing like the same quality of wines as Argentina and Chile.

Mexico

Although it was the first country in the Americas to produce wine, 400 years ago, Mexico has never developed a fully fledged wine industry. The best vineyards are just inside the Mexican border in Baja California, where some good, robust reds are made from grapes such as Cabernet, Nebbiolo and Petite Sirah. Its wines have potential, though the home market is keener on tequila.

Below: Irrigation canal in one of Chile's major wine regions, the Curico Valley.

Australia

No country has done more to entice new wine-drinkers than Australia. With its easy-to-understand grape varieties, generously fruity flavors, and ability to turn out reliably consistent wines vintage after vintage, it's all anyone new to wine could wish for.

But, in fact, Australia is not quite what it seems. Despite all the hype and the excitement it has generated, it is, in fact, still a small wine-producing country. Not geographically of course (the distance from Sydney to Perth is the same as from London to Moscow), but small in terms of volume. To put it in proportion, Australia still only accounts for just over two percent of the world's total wine production – about a twelfth the amount of Italy. But, what wine Australia does produce is of outstandingly high quality.

A distinctive approach

One of the reasons it has made so much impact is that we tend to think of "Australian wine" rather than wine from individual regions. And indeed that's the way the Australians make it. Instead of seeking to reflect the unique character of a specific area, Australian producers take their grapes not only from different regions but different states, trucking them vast distances to be blended together. Even some of Australia's best wines – such as Penfolds' Grange – are made this way, the argument being that it enables wine-makers to select the very best grapes available to them, no matter where they come from. But, in fact, there are quite significant differences between the states – and regions within states – that more and more producers (and the wine authorities) are seeking to reflect.

Main wine regions

Australia's wine regions are surprisingly varied. Some are cool. Some are blindingly hot. Some, such as the Clare Valley near Adelaide, are both. Australia is still a young wine-producing country and is only just beginning to identify the vineyards that best suit the grape varieties they want to grow.

Southeast Australia

This catch-all description means that the grapes used to make the wine may have come from any one of three states – South Australia, Victoria or New South Wales – or from all three. Most come from the so-called Riverlands – huge tracts of irrigated land in each of the three states. These supply two-thirds of Australia's wine and account for most of the grapes that go into well-known brands such as Jacob's Creek, Bin 65 and Nottage Hill.

South Australia

This area, centred around Adelaide, is the heart of the modern Australian wine industry, accounting for half its production and most of its top wines. South Australia's trademark is its big, full-bodied reds, the best of which come from the Barossa Valley, Coonawarra and McLaren Vale. It also produces some of Australia's best whites – Riesling, from the Clare and Eden Valleys, Semillon, Sauvignon and

Chardonnay – the finest of which tend to be made in the cooler areas around the Adelaide Hills and Padthaway.

Victoria

The state of Victoria was once more important than it is now but went into decline after its vineyards were struck by phylloxera. Although, like other regions, the bulk of its wines come from the Riverland vineyards that border the Murray River, it's more notable for its quirkier wines – Marsanne, a Semillon-like grape, that grows in the Goulbourn Valley, some massively concentrated reds and Australia's great fortified wine, liqueur Muscat. Its most prestigious region is the Yarra Valley, a comparatively cool area that produces fine Chardonnay, Pinot Noir and sparkling wine, but could be rivalled by the up-and-coming areas of Bendigo, Geelong and the Mornington Peninsula. Just off the coast of Victoria is Tasmania, the coolest winegrowing region in Australia; again, most notable for high-quality Pinot Noir and Chardonnay.

New South Wales

The most famous wine region in New South Wales is the Hunter Valley – one of the earliest wine regions to be developed and, as most Australians freely admit, one of the most difficult to cultivate because of its high levels of humidity and rainfall. That said, it does produce two of the country's most distinctive wines – a particularly farmyardy, leathery style of Shiraz, and the most incredibly long-lived Semillon (*see* pages 56–9). It could be eclipsed in future by the promising new areas of Mudgee and Orange.

Above: Vineyard in the Great Western district of Victoria, old gold-rush country.

Western Australia

Western Australia is the Burgundy of Australia, with a reputation out of proportion to its size. Although hot, its climate is much more temperate than southern Australia, and its wines (chiefly Chardonnay, Cabernet, Merlot and Shiraz) more elegant and classically European in style. The two key areas are the Margaret River and Lower Great Southern (the name you more commonly see on a label is Mount Barker) but some good, less expensive whites, such as HWB (Houghton's White Burgundy), come from the Swan Valley.

Where the best wines come from

As the Australian wine industry has become more sophisticated, certain regions have become associated with particular grape varieties.

Australian whites

Chardonnay – this often depends as much on the style of the winemaker as where it comes from. Top Australian Chardonnays are generally rich and full-bodied, but lighter, more European styles come from the Margaret River, Yarra Valley and Tasmania.

Riesling – the star areas are the Clare and Eden Valleys, producing a particularly rich, limey style of Riesling, that develops intriguing petrolly notes as it ages.

Semillon – traditional unoaked Semillons (often as low as 10 percent in alcohol) come from the Hunter Valley. More modern styles come from the Barossa and Clare Valleys.

Sauvignon Blanc – not the ideal grape for Australia (it's too hot), but there are good examples from the Adelaide Hills, particularly the Lenswood area.

Australian reds

Shiraz – at its distinctive peppery best in the Barossa Valley, richer and lusher in the Clare Valley and McLaren Vale. Hunter Valley Shiraz traditionally has what is described as a "sweaty saddle" (i.e. a slightly animal, leathery character), but nowadays is fruitier. Margaret River Shiraz is much softer and smoother.

Cabernet Sauvignon – Cabernet from the Coonawarra region has a particularly characteristic eucalyptus style (*see* pages 70–1), but other southern Australian Cabernets are pretty minty too. Margaret River and Mount Barker Cabernets are lighter and more elegant, though equally ripe.

Right: Close-up of the *terra rossa* soil in South Australia's Coonawarra region, brick-red earth above deep limestone.

Grenache and Mourvèdre – thrive in the same areas as Shiraz – the Barossa and Clare Valleys and McLaren Vale. Anywhere it's really hot.

Pinot Noir – does well in the same cool areas as Chardonnay – the Yarra Valley, Geelong, Tasmania and the Margaret River.

For more information on Australian wine styles and grape varieties, *see* pages 12–23 and 56–75.

Stickies

"Stickies" is a brilliantly appropriate word to describe Australia's unique style of fortified wine, liqueur Muscat, deliciously rich, and treacly, tasting just like liquid Christmas pudding. The last legacy from Australia's fortified wine-making past, liqueur Muscat is made in the Rutherglen area of Victoria. Australia also produces port-style wines that are not allowed to be called "port" (when exported anyway), and some remarkably inexpensive dessert wines from botrytised Riesling and Semillon.

Sparkling wines

Like its still wines, Australian sparkling wines offer breezy, uncomplicated drinking. With one or two exceptions (such as Moët et Chandon's Green Point), they don't even attempt to rival Champagne. Most are made from Chardonnay and are much fruitier than the traditional yeasty style favored by winemakers elsewhere. There are also a significant number of light, strawberry-flavored rosés and sparkling reds, such as sparkling Shiraz or Grenache – dark red, frothy concoctions of ripe berry fruits, that are utterly and exuberantly over the top.

Reading Australian labels

Australian wine labels – like Australian wines – are wonderfully straightforward. There are no complicated rules and regulations as there are in many parts of Europe that dictate what information must be put on the label. What you see is what you get. The front label will generally tell you the grape variety or varieties the wine is made from, the name of the producer, the region the wine comes from and the alcohol content. But there's normally also additional information on the back of the bottle that tells you more about the style of wine, the kind of food it goes with, how long you can keep it and – where it's an important feature of the wine – the way it was made (*see* also page 81).

These three labels are all different wines produced by Australia's largest producer, Southcorp. The first, Seaview, is an inexpensive, light sparkling wine – you can see that the alcohol content is only 11 percent. Keeping their options open, the producers only say that it is Australian – it could have come from any part of Southeast Australia. No grape variety is mentioned either, just the word "brut", which indicates that it is dry.

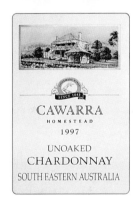

This label is more specific. It says that the wine comes from Southeast Australia. It tells you the variety is Chardonnay and that it's unoaked, indicating that this is a lighter, fruitier style of wine. Cawarra is the brand name of the wine, which is named (so the back label tells us) after the first vineyards planted by the company's founder, Dr Henry John Lindeman (New World producers like to wrap themselves in a bit of history). But essentially this is a typical, modern, mass-market brand.

Quite often Australian wines have "bin" numbers on them. Originally this was a device for keeping different batches of grapes apart. These days production is on a much larger scale, so this wine no longer comes from a single vineyard but from various parts of South Australia, the aim being to get a consistent blend from year to year. The fact that it is made from just one grape variety, Shiraz, is also an indication of quality. Shiraz is an expensive grape variety and many of the grapes used will have come from low-yielding old vines.

New Zealand

For a small wine-producing country, New Zealand punches well above its weight. In an astonishingly short time (less than 30 years) it has become one of the New World's most serious players. Yet, it only accounts for a minute percentage of the world's wine production.

But, that shouldn't lead you into thinking that New Zealand's wines are all the same. Although it has based its reputation on one style of wine – a gloriously intense style of Sauvignon – its vineyards span a distance of some 1,500 miles, making them as far apart as Germany and Algeria.

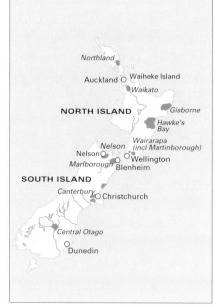

The North Island

Much warmer than the South Island, the North Island is almost tropical in parts. Most wineries are based around Auckland (even if they don't source their grapes from there), which has a warm and humid temperature, similar to Australia's Hunter Valley. But within half an hour's ferry ride is the cult island of Waiheke, where you get much drier and less-humid conditions, resulting in the production of some of the country's best reds.

The most important wine-producing areas of the North Island are Gisborne and Hawke's Bay on the east coast, both comparatively hot. Gisborne is noted for its whites, particularly Chardonnay, Hawke's Bay for its Bordeaux-style reds, although it makes excellent Chardonnay too. At the cooler, southernmost tip of the island is Martinborough, a tiny region, that has established a world-class reputation for Pinot Noir.

The South Island

Right at the top of the South Island is Marlborough, New Zealand's biggest and most prestigious wine-growing area, home to the fabled Cloudy Bay and many other top producers. Although it's a cool area, it's also sunny, which results in long, slow ripening conditions, that give its whites a tremendous intensity of flavor. As well as Sauvignon Blanc,

Above: Autumn color sweeps across the Brancott Estate Vineyards in Marlborough.

it produces top-quality Chardonnay, Riesling, sparkling wine and, more recently, Pinot Noir. Also to the north is Nelson, which has a similar climate to Marlborough. Then, quite a bit farther south are two cooler growing regions, Canterbury and Central Otago, both noted for their Pinot Noir.

New Zealand whites

New Zealand produces much more white wine than red, a lot of it being inexpensive, fresh, floral, medium-dry white. Although it is famous for its Sauvignon, New Zealand produces more Chardonnay, which ranges from the ripe peachy flavors of Gisborne Chardonnay, to the lighter, more citrussy styles you find in Marlborough. Because of its comparatively high levels of acidity it ages well – better on the whole than Chardonnay from Australia.

Sauvignon itself has evolved. It's still piercingly intense but with less of the gooseberry and asparagus character it used to have, and more ripe tropical fruit flavors.

New Zealand is also having considerable success with aromatic grapes such as Gewürztraminer, Pinot Gris and Riesling, which are often made in a similarly rich style to those of Alsace. Chenin Blanc can be good too.

New Zealand reds

Until recently New Zealand's reds were a disappointment. Originally, growers chose to plant Cabernet, but have found it consistently hard to ripen the grape. In Hawke's Bay winemakers tend to blend it with Merlot, Cabernet Franc and Malbec to make softer, more supple reds. In the

Marlborough region winemakers are switching to Pinot Noir, which they believe can do for the country's reds what Sauvignon Blanc did for its whites.

Sweet wines and sparklers

Although New Zealand's sweet wines, which are mainly based on Riesling, are not widely available, they are stunning. New Zealand is also a high-quality producer of sparkling wine, made in the Champagne style and, in a number of cases, with the help of the Champagne producers themselves.

Above: The Richmond Ranges viewed from vineyards in the Wairau River Valley.

Small is beautiful

New Zealand wines can be expensive, but most of its winemakers are really small. Take out the four biggest wine companies (Montana, Villa Maria, Corbans and Nobilo) and the country's remaining 250-odd producers account for just ten percent of its production. The pay-off is quality. Most of New Zealand's whites are world class and the reds are on their way.

South Africa

Because of its turbulent political history, South Africa has been a relative latecomer on world markets, slow to realize its undoubted potential. But, surprisingly, it has been producing wine since Dutch settlers arrived in the mid 17th century.

Most of the vineyards are concentrated in the southwest of the country, around Cape Town. They're divided up into recognized wine regions but these don't have a very clear identity. Paarl, for example, produces a lot of inexpensive wines, but also contains some serious producers such as Fairview, Glen Carlou and Villiera. The same is true of Robertson. The most distinctive regions are Stellenbosch, which produces most of the country's best reds, and the cool coastal areas of Walker Bay and Constantia, where boutique winemakers produce some fine Burgundian-style Chardonnay and Pinot Noir.

Small producers are in the minority, however. The industry is still dominated by cooperatives, the best known of which is the Kooperative Wijnbouwers Vereniging (KWV), established in 1917, which until recently controlled not only what grapes should be planted, but how much growers should be paid for them.

Above: Rustenberg, an old Stellenbosch estate in the classic Cape Dutch style.

What South Africa has to offer

Like most of the New World, the emphasis here is on internationally planted grape varieties such as Chardonnay, Cabernet and Merlot.

Although the climate is hot, South African wines don't tend to have the exuberant up-front fruitiness of those from Australia or Chile, and many of them even taste quite European in style.

The best guide to style is price. The vast majority of those that are exported are inexpensive – decent, but often quite dull. The most interesting wines are those in the medium-to-expensive price bracket from quality producers (comparing favorably in price to top wines from countries such as Australia, New Zealand and California). Names to look for include Bouchard Finlayson, Neil Ellis, Hamilton Russell, Grangehurst, Jordan, Klein Constantia, La Motte, Thelema and Warwick.

South African whites

Surprisingly, 85 percent of the wine South Africa produces is white, most of it Chenin Blanc (known here as Steen) and Colombard. Chenin produces smooth, dry, melony whites, as opposed to the crisp, green-apple fruit you find in the Loire, the best wines coming from older "bush vines." Sauvignon also does particularly well, producing piercingly crisp, minerally, wines that can rival Sancerre for quality.

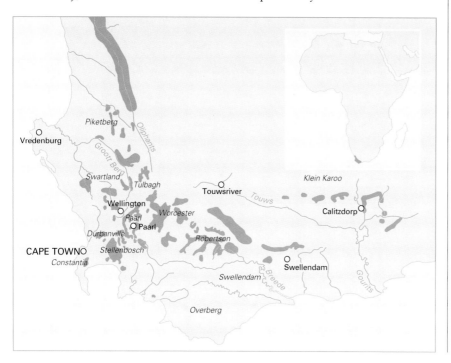

Chardonnay veers between restrained, classic styles and more exuberantly oaky ones, but is competitively priced compared with other similar New-World wines. The grape to watch, though, is Sémillon, which shows every sign of becoming a new star for South Africa.

South African reds

Like California, South Africa has modeled its serious reds on Bordeaux. Blends of Cabernet Sauvignon with Merlot and Cabernet Franc often work better than Cabernet on its own, though there are some good rich Merlots. And coastal areas, such as Walker Bay, produce some fine Pinot Noir.

Winemakers have also had success with fuller-bodied reds such as Shiraz, Zinfandel, and especially Pinotage – the country's most distinctive grape variety. Pinotage's odd name reflects its origins as a cross between Pinot Noir and Cinsault (formerly known as Hermitage). Like Australia's Shiraz and California's Zinfandel it can be made in a number of different styles, from light and juicy, to rich, full-bodied and plummy – the latter being by far the most interesting. Winemaker Beyers Truter of Kanonkop is a name to look for.

Cheaper reds (not South Africa's strength) tend to be made from blends of Cinsault, Pinotage and Ruby Cabernet, though Tinta Barroca, a variety traditionally used for port, can make much gutsier examples.

Sparkling wines

South Africa has its own name for its Champagne-style sparkling wines – Méthode Cap Classique. They tend to be less elegant than Champagne and top Australian and Californian sparklers, but they offer very good value for the money.

Fortified and sweet wines

Two centuries ago South Africa's great sweet wine, Constantia, was one of the most sought-after dessert wines in the world. One or two producers, including Klein Constantia, have attempted a replica, but these days winemakers are more interested in producing modern late-harvest-style wines from grapes such as Riesling and Sémillon.

South Africans also produce some excellent sherry- and port-style wines. Look for delicious, richly toffeed Jerepigo and warm, sweet, brambly Muscadel.

Early Release Chenin Blanc

As Chenin Blanc matures early it has taken over from Beaujolais the distinction of producing the first wine of the calendar year, generally reaching the shelves by May or June. Demand comes mainly from the British market where there is an inexhaustible appetite for anything new and different. Most are made by visiting Australian winemakers and are exuberantly fruity in style. Look for the expression "Early Release Chenin" on the label.

Below: The Haute Cabrière Estate in Franschhoek, which has some of the best vineyards in the Paarl region.

The rest of the winemaking world

It's amazing how many countries actually produce wine, even in the most unpromising conditions. In tropical climates, such as those in India and Bangladesh, vines can produce two harvests a year, which really rules them out of the big league in quality terms. But even these two countries have cool enough areas to make grape-growing viable.

A bigger handicap can be the prevailing religion and culture. Muslim countries, such as Algeria and Turkey, have the right climate to be successful wine producers, but with a largely teetotal population there's little incentive to invest in quality wine.

Northern Europe

England and Wales

Global warming has undoubtedly done Great Britain a favor in winemaking terms. Successive hot summers during the 1990s have done much to help English and Welsh winemakers in their bid to be taken seriously. They deserve to be. Standards have improved greatly since the days when England only produced dull, Germanic-style, medium-dry whites, with new crosses of grapes such as Bacchus and Ortega producing some really stylish crisp wines. There are even some impressive, soft, plummy reds. But Britain's best hope may lie in producing quality sparkling wine – the climate and soil in the southeast of England is very similar to Champagne.

Other countries

Luxembourg is the largest of northern Europe's other producers, though vines are also grown in Holland, Belgium and Denmark.

Below: Pinot Noir vineyard and the winery and visitors' center of Denbies Estate in Dorking, Surrey. With 250 acres of vines, it is the largest wine estate in England.

The Eastern Mediterranean

Greece

Greece could be the next big discovery of the wine world, somewhat ironically, as it's been making wine longer than anyone else. The country's hot climate is particularly conducive to making full-bodied reds, with winemakers combining local grapes such as Agiorgitiko (St-George) and Xynomavro, with international varieties including Cabernet Sauvignon. Some impressive Chardonnays are emerging too – good news for those of us who've never been won over by Greece's curious pine-flavored white, Retsina.

It's also worth looking for some of Greece's excellent, Muscat-based dessert wines, particularly those from the islands of Samos and Santorini; and its delicious, inexpensive, sweet, port-like red, Mavrodaphne of Patras.

Other countries

The Lebanon is famous for one extraordinary wine, Chateau Musar, a fine, ageworthy red based on Cabernet and Cinsault, that continued to be produced right through the Civil War. There is a well-developed (largely white) wine-industry in Israel, that satisfies worldwide demand for kosher wines. Wine is also produced in Cyprus and Turkey, but in neither country to a particularly high standard.

North and central Africa

The French colonial presence in the north of Africa has left a legacy of winemaking expertise in Algeria, Morocco and Tunisia. Morocco's vigorous, brambly reds are the ones that most regularly find their way into export markets. Made from southern

French grape varieties such as Cinsault, Grenache and Syrah, they're not the subtlest of wines, but .a suitably robust accompaniment to the country's exotic and spicy cuisine. Limited amounts of wine are also produced in Kenya and Zimbabwe.

Asia

With the growing interest in wine in the Far East, it's not surprising that several countries are attempting to make some of their own, though the tropical climate in places such as India and Bangladesh doesn't make the enterprise easy. Japan so far leads the field in quality terms, with the backing of big companies such

Above: Vines protected against cold winter weather in the Nagano region, central Honshu, Japan.

as Sapporo Suntory and Kikkoman, all of whom own wineries. Japan also has independent producers who are making Bordeaux-style reds from Cabernet and Merlot.

Parts of China also have a climate that is suitable for grape growing and is attracting a fair amount of foreign investment. Again the focus is mainly on internationally grown varieties, such as Chardonnay, while India's best-known wine is, surprisingly, a sparkling one, Omar Khayyam.

Flavor crib

Here's a key to the flavors you'll find on the flavor wheel.

FRUITY

Apple Green apples: crisp-dry whites, Mosel Kabinett Riesling. Stewed apple: softer whites such as Fumé Blanc and lighter styles of Chardonnay.

Pear Chenin Blanc. The aroma of peardrops (which can also smell like nail polish or bubblegum) is also found in young wines such as Beaujolais.

Lemon Crisp dry whites. In riper New World wines such as Sémillon and Sauvignon the flavor is more lemon peel than lemon juice.

Grapefruit Crisper styles of Chardonnay, Scheurebe.

Orange Many sweet Muscats, particularly Orange Muscat. Marsala.

Lime Australian Riesling, Sémillon, New Zealand Sauvignon Blanc.

Gooseberry Sauvignon Blanc.

Grape Muscat, German Riesling.

Pineapple Fresh: ultra-ripe Chardonnays and Sémillon. Roast/caramelized: older Sémillon and Marsanne.

Melon Lighter styles of Chardonnay, Chenin Blanc.

Banana Beaujolais Nouveau and other newly made wines.

Peach Chardonnay, white Bordeaux, botrytized dessert wines.

Apricot Viognier.

Mango New World Chardonnay and Sémillon.

Lychee Gewürztraminer, Irsai Oliver.

Cherry Valpolicella, Beaujolais and other light, fruity reds.

Strawberry Pinot Noir Rosé, younger Pinot Noirs.

Raspberry Young Pinot Noir, Cabernet Franc, Beaujolais.

Plum Fresh: Merlot, Zinfandel. Cooked: vintage port.

Blackberry Many red wines including Bordeaux.

Blackcurrant Cabernet Sauvignon.

Raisin Sweet oloroso sherry, Malmsey, liqueur Muscat.

Prune Southern Italian reds.

Fig Similar to raisin.

Jam Strawberry jam: Grenache, Rioja. Blackcherry/blackcurrant jam: Full-bodied New World reds.

SWEET

Chocolate Richer styles of red, particularly Merlot and Shiraz.

Toffee Australian liqueur Muscats, amontillado sherry.

Butterscotch Big, barrel-fermented Chardonnays.

Honey Vouvray, aged Chenin Blanc, vintage Champagne, Sauternes.

WOOD

Vanilla Oaked Chardonnays, Rioja and other traditional Spanish reds.

Oak Newly released oaked (or oak chipped) whites and reds.

Cedar Red Bordeaux and other top Cabernet Sauvignons.

SPICE

Tobacco Red Bordeaux.

Smoke Pouilly-Fumé, Syrah. Can also come from heavily charred barrels.

Licorice Big, full-bodied reds such as Zinfandel.

Pepper White pepper: Gruner Veltliner, Cabernet Franc. Black pepper: Syrah and Shiraz.

Cinnamon Mature Syrah.

SAVORY

Ground coffee Top quality Bordeaux and Italian reds.

Leather Old-fashioned Hunter Valley Shiraz, aged Rhône reds.

Bacon Big, savory reds such as Syrah from the Rhône and Pinotage. Game Mature red Burgundy and other aged Pinot Noir.

Truffles Aged Pinot Noir.

HERBAL

Eucalyptus Southern Australian Cabernet Sauvignon.

Mint New World Cabernet Sauvignon, some Australian Shiraz.

Green (bell) pepper Cabernet Sauvignon and Cabernet Franc.

Asparagus Sauvignon Blanc.

Cut grass Sauvignon Blanc and Sauvignon-style wines.

Hay Vintage Champagne.

FLORAL

Blossom Mosel Riesling, Viognier.

Elderflowers Muscat.

Red roses Gewürztraminer. Sometimes there's a touch in Pinot Noir.

Violets Top-quality red Bordeaux; Syrah, particularly Côte-Rôtie. Also top Chinon and Bourgueil; top Pinot Noir.

NUTTY

Almonds Soave, Bianco di Custoza and similar dry Italian whites.

Biscuits Vintage Champagne.

Grilled nuts Top white burgundy, vintage Champagne, drier styles of sherry, tawny port.

Toast Barrel-fermented Chardonnay, vintage Champagne.

Bread Non-vintage Champagne.

Yeast Muscadet and drier styles of Champagne. Fino and manzanilla sherry.

DAIRY

Cream Richer styles of Chardonnay and Chenin Blanc.

Butter Richer styles of Chardonnay, especially ones that have undergone malolactic fermentation (*see* page 81).

MINERAL

Petrol Mature Riesling.

Earth Ultra-dry whites such as Muscadet, and traditional southern French whites.

Stones Dry Italian whites.

Flint Chablis; Sancerre and other Loire Sauvignons.

Tasting terms

Acidity
More desirable than it sounds. Without acidity – a slight sharpness – wines would taste flat and flabby. Particularly characteristic of crisp, dry whites such as Sauvignon.

Balanced
A wine with all its elements – fruit, oak and tannin – in balance and is therefore easy to drink.

Bouquet/Nose
Technical taster's term for what a wine smells like.

Clean
A wine that is technically irreproachable but not very demanding. Usually used for cheaper wines to indicate qualified approval. Can also be called correct.

Closed
A wine that doesn't smell or taste of much, but has potential. Sometimes a young wine needs time for its flavors to develop. Other wines, such as aromatic or sweet wines, can go through a "closed" period when they temporarily become less interesting.

Complex
A wine that has several intermingling flavors rather than one that is simply fruity.

Crisp
Indicates a high level of acidity. Used for lighter styles of whites.

Dry
Potentially misleading as what is dry to one person may not taste dry to another. Almost anything that isn't medium-dry is referred to as dry.

Earthy
Literally that. A slightly earthy flavor you pick up on some wines, often due to the strong influence of the soil. More attractive than it sounds.

Elegant
A fine wine in a lighter style – i.e. not an oaky blockbuster. Could also be described as classy or stylish.

Fat
A compliment in wine terms. Generally used for full-bodied wines such as Chardonnay and Sémillon that have a slightly syrupy texture.

Finish
The sensation that's left in your mouth when you swallow, i.e. the aftertaste.

Firm
Well structured. Mainly used for reds to indicate a capacity to age.

Fleshy
Description used of particularly lush, fruity wines.

Floral
Perfumed Used for aromatic whites such as Riesling and Viognier.

Food Wine
Slightly double-edged. Means not a wine you would necessarily choose to drink on its own, but generally used approvingly for slightly neutral wines that come into their own with food.

Forward
The term used by professional winetasters to indicate a wine whose flavors are more pronounced or obvious than you would expect for its age. Generous A (usually red) wine with warm, sweet, ripe fruit flavors.

Herbaceous
A green, herbal, grassy type of flavor. Often used for Sauvignon and Sauvignon-style wines but sometimes (less complimentarily) for Cabernet Sauvignon.

Jammy
Indicates particularly lush, red fruit flavors. Usually used for New World wines by people who think the wines are too sweet.

Lean
A very dry wine or one that tastes a bit thin.

Legs
A term used by professional tasters to refer to the syrupy streaks that run down the glass after a wine has been swirled. Tends to be more obvious in wines that are high in alcohol or are very sweet. Sometimes referred to as "tears."

Length
The persistence of the taste. A wine that lingers in your mouth after you have swallowed it is described as "long in the mouth." One that fades quickly is "short."

Lively

Crisp and fresh. Used for lighter reds and whites.

New World

Shorthand for the particularly vivid styles of wine that emerge from countries such as Australia and Chile. (As opposed to Old World, which describes more European styles of wine.)

Palate

Used in two ways: what the wine actually tastes like in the mouth (on the palate), and for whether someone is a good taster (e.g. he/she has a good palate.)

Robust

Indicates a wine that is full of flavor but probably not hugely subtle. Generally used for cheaper, full-bodied reds that also may be described as "gutsy."

Rounded

Smooth and easy to drink.

Silky

Particularly fine-textured wines that feel almost silky in the mouth. Used mainly for red burgundy and other top-quality Pinot Noir.

Soft

Used principally for reds that have no harsh tannins or marked acidity.

Spicy

A flavor you generally pick up on the aftertaste. Usually the result of oak but some grape varieties, such as Gewürztraminer, Syrah and Zinfandel, are particularly spicy.

Steely

Very dry, and not at all fruity. Mainly used for younger, unoaked styles of Chablis.

Structure

A wine that offers more than an instant hit is described as well-structured. It usually indicates that it has the ability to age.

Supple

Used with approval to indicate a red wine that is smooth, fruity and well balanced – as opposed to one that is more tannic.

Tannic

Harsh, slightly unyielding – though wines that are tannic in their youth often age well. Used for red wines.

Varietal character

A wine that is typical of the grape variety from which it is made shows varietal character. Tasters also talk about typicity.

Vinous

A wine that tastes of wine. A term you'd think would apply to all wines but which tends to be applied to more traditional, less fruity styles.

Young/youthful

Slightly double-edged. Can refer approvingly to the fact that a wine tastes fresh and fruity, but may also indicate that there are some slightly harsh flavors that the taster doesn't approve of, or which will take time to integrate.

Index

Publisher Acknowledgments
The publisher would like to thank the following for their generosity
in providing wines and props for use in the photography in this book.
Majestic Wine Warehouses for the wine photographed in the grape tasting section
Oddbins for wines tasted by the author in her research for the grape tasting section
Michael Johnson Ceramics for the use of Riedel glasses

Ogetti for the use of the stainless steel corkscrew on the jacket
Champagne Lanson
Colored, laminated wine aroma wheels are available from AC Noble,
Dept Viticulture and Enology, University of California, Davis, CA 95616 USA.
Fax (530) 752 0382. Email acnoble@ucdavis.edu. All profits support wine
sensory research at UCD.

Author Acknowledgments
Three groups of people deserve heartfelt thanks. First all the people
in the business whose knowledge I plundered including Hazel Murphy of the
Australian Wine Bureau, Phil Reedman of Tesco (formerly of the ustralian
Wine Club), John McLaren of Wines of California, Ginny Martin of Sopexa,
Charlotte Hey from Wines from Spain, Barbara and James from the German
Wine Information Service, Lisa McGovern of the New Zealand Wine Guild,

Burton Anderson, and John Ritchie of Valvona & Crolla. Next, the home
team at Mitchell Beazley – the wondrously efficient Lucy (whose elegant
likeness you can see on pages 52–3) Margaret and Becca (for being
outrageously good company as well as inspirational editors) and Fiona
and Clive for making the book so great to look at. And last, but not least,
my family, especially Trevor whose love, advice and support I couldn't
do without.

Picture Credits
Acknowledgements in Page Order
Key: Octopus Publishing Group – OPG
 Cephas Picture Library – Cephas

Front Jacket OPG Ltd/James Johnson
Back cover OPG Ltd/Steven Morris Back flap Guy Drayton

2 OPG Ltd/Martin Brigdale, 4-5 OPG Ltd/James Johnson, 6-7 OPG Ltd/Richard McConnell, 8 OPG Ltd/James Johnson, 10-11 OPG Ltd/Ray Moller, 12 OPG Ltd/Ray Moller, 13 OPG Ltd/James Johnson, 14 OPG Ltd/James Johnson, 15 top OPG Ltd/James Johnson, 15 bottom OPG Ltd/Ray Moller, 16 OPG Ltd/Ray Moller, 17 OPG Ltd/James Johnson, 18 OPG Ltd/James Johnson, 19 left OPG Ltd/Steven Morris, 19 right OPG Ltd/Ray Moller, 20 OPG Ltd/Ray Moller, 21 OPG Ltd/Steven Morris, 22 OPG Ltd/Ray Moller, 23 OPG Ltd/James Johnson, 24-25 OPG Ltd/Kim Sayer, 26 Cephas/Mick Rock, 27 Cephas/Mick Rock, 29 OPG Ltd, 30 OPG Ltd/Ray Moller, 31 OPG Ltd/James Johnson, 33 OPG Ltd/Jeremy Hopley, 34 OPG Ltd/Ray Moller, 37 top left OPG Ltd/Laurie Evans, 37 top right OPG Ltd/Laurie Evans, 37 bottom left OPG Ltd/Laurie Evans, 37 bottom right OPG Ltd/Ray Moller, 38 top left OPG Ltd/Ray Moller, 38 top right OPG Ltd/Jeremy Hopley, 38 bottom left OPG Ltd/Ray Moller, 38 bottom right OPG Ltd/Jeremy Hopley, 41 OPG Ltd/Joe Cornish, 42 Oddbins Ltd/Wilson Photographics, 43 Oddbins Ltd, 44 OPG Ltd/Ray Moller, 45 left OPG Ltd/Ray Moller, 45 centre OPG Ltd/James Johnson, 46 OPG Ltd/Ray Moller, 47 OPG Ltd/James Johnson 48 Anthony Blake Photo Library, 50 OPG Ltd/Steven Morris, 51 OPG Ltd/Ray Moller, 52 OPG Ltd/Ray Moller, 53 OPG Ltd/Ray Moller, 54-55 OPG Ltd/David Harrison, 56 Cephas/Mick Rock, 57 top Cephas/Kevin Judd, 57 bottom Cephas/Mick Rock, 58 Cephas/Mick Rock, 59 top Cephas/Ted Stefan 59 bottom Cephas/Mick Rock, 60 OPG Ltd/James Johnson, 61 top left OPG Ltd/Ray Moller, 61 top centre OPG Ltd/James Johnson, 61 top centre right OPG Ltd/Ray Moller, 61 top right OPG Ltd/Ray Moller, 61 bottom left OPG Ltd/James Johnson, 61 bottom right OPG Ltd/James Johnson, 62 OPG Ltd/James Johnson, 63 top left OPG Ltd/James Johnson, 63 top centre OPG Ltd/James Johnson, 63 top right OPG Ltd/Ray Moller, 63 bottom left OPG Ltd/James Johnson, 63 bottom right OPG Ltd/James Johnson, 64 OPG Ltd/James Johnson, 65 top left OPG Ltd/James Johnson, 65 top centre OPG Ltd/Ray Moller, 65 top right OPG Ltd/Ray Moller, 65 bottom left OPG Ltd/James Johnson, 65 bottom right OPG Ltd/James Johnson, 66 Cephas/Mick Rock, 67 Cephas/Mick Rock, 68 Cephas/Mick Rock, 69 Cephas/Mick Rock, 70 OPG Ltd/James Johnson, 71 top left OPG Ltd/James Johnson, 71 top centre OPG Ltd/James Johnson, 71 top right OPG Ltd/Ray Moller, 71 bottom left OPG Ltd/James Johnson, 71 bottom right OPG Ltd/James Johnson, 72 OPG Ltd/James Johnson, 73 top left OPG Ltd/James Johnson, 73 top centre OPG Ltd/James Johnson, 73 top right OPG Ltd/Ray Moller, 73 bottom left OPG Ltd/James Johnson, 73 bottom right OPG Ltd/James Johnson, 74 OPG Ltd/James Johnson, 75 top left OPG Ltd/James Johnson, 75 top centre OPG Ltd/James Johnson, 75 top right OPG Ltd/Ray Moller, 75 bottom left OPG Ltd/James Johnson, 75 bottom right OPG Ltd/James Johnson, 76 Cephas/Mick Rock, 77 Cephas/Mick Rock, 78 Cephas/Mick Rock, 79 Cephas/Mick Rock 80 Cephas/Mick Rock, 81 Cephas/Mick Rock, 82 Cephas/Mick Rock, 83 Cephas/Alain Proust, 84 OPG Ltd/James Johnson, 85 top left OPG Ltd/Ray Moller, 85 top centre OPG Ltd/James Johnson, 85 top right Garden Picture Library/JS Sira, 85 bottom left OPG Ltd/James Johnson, 85 bottom right OPG Ltd/James Johnson, 86-87 Christie's Images, 91 Cephas/Mick Rock, 92 Cephas/Mick Rock, 95 Cephas/Mick Rock, 96 Cephas/Mick Rock, 97 Cephas/Mick Rock, 98 Scope/Jean-Luc Barde, 99 Skalli, 100 Cephas/Mick Rock 101 Cephas/Mick Rock, 102 Scope/Jacques Guillard, 105 Root Stock/Hendrik Holler, 106 Cephas/Mick Rock, 107 Root Stock/Hendrik Holler, 109 Root Stock/Hendrik Holler, 110 Anthony Blake Photo Library/John Sims, 111 OPG Ltd/Alan Williams, 113 Root Stock/Hendrik Holler, 114 Cephas/Mick Rock, 116 Robert Harding Picture Library/James Strachan, 119 Root Stock/Hendrik Holler, 121 Cephas/Ted Stefanski, 122 Cephas/Mick Rock, 123 Scope/Sara Matthews, 125 Cephas/Andy Christodolo, 127 Root Stock/Hendrik Holler, 128 Root Stock/Hendrik Holler, 129 top OPG Ltd/Seaview, 129 centre OPG Ltd/Cawarra, 129 bottom OPG Ltd/Penfolds, 130 Cephas/Kevin Judd, 131 Cephas/Kevin Judd, 132 Root Stock/Hendrik Holler, 133 Root Stock/Hendrik Holler, 134 Cephas/Mick Rock, 135 Cephas/Nigel Blythe